WELCOME

For the Allied powers, the route to victory during the Second World War was far from a straight one. Between the outbreak of the war in 1939, to the darkest days of 1940, the Axis alliance of Italy, Japan and Germany went almost undefeated in their conquests across the globe. However, through determined strategy, technical innovation, and diplomatic guile, the Allies eventually united to forge a triumphant path to victory by 1945. From major military turning points, to world-changing events, it's a path you can retrace over the following pages.

★ CONTENTS ★

★ 1941-42 ★

06	ATLANTIC CONFERENCE
08	SECOND BATTLE OF EL ALAMEIN
12	MIDWAY
16	GUADALCANAL
20	MOSCOW CONFERENCE
22	ILYUSHIN IL-2 SHTURMOVIK
28	STALINGRAD
32	ARCTIC CONVOYS

★ 1943 ★

36	CASABLANCA CONFERENCE
38	INVASION OF SICILY
42	SUPERMARINE SPITFIRE
46	BLACK MAY 1943
50	T-34 MEDIUM TANK
56	PROKHOROVKA
60	TEHRAN CONFERENCE

96

62

106

★ 1944 ★

62	LIBERATION OF ROME
64	MONTE CASSINO
68	MUSSOLINI'S DOWNFALL
72	D-DAY
74	LCVP HIGGINS BOAT
76	SWORD BEACH
80	RED BALL EXPRESS
82	SHERMAN FIREFLY
88	BATTLE OF THE PHILIPPINES
92	OPERATION BAGRATION

38

1945

96	YALTA CONFERENCE
98	VISTULA-ODER OFFENSIVE
102	WILLYS JEEP
104	LUNEBURG HEATH SURRENDER
106	BATTLE OF BERLIN
112	SURRENDER OF GERMANY
114	BURMA CAMPAIGN
118	IWO JIMA
122	HIROSHIMA
126	SURRENDER OF JAPAN

Roosevelt (left) and Churchill attend the Sunday church service on HMS Prince of Wales during the Atlantic Conference

★ 9 AUGUST 1941 ★

THE ATLANTIC CONFERENCE

President Franklin D Roosevelt and Prime Minister Winston Churchill met to discuss common ground in the fight against Axis aggression

WORDS **MICHAEL E HASKEW**

In 1941, British Prime Minister Winston Churchill led a nation at war, standing alone against the might of Nazi Germany. President Franklin D Roosevelt had extended aid as best his government was able in the face of strong isolationist sentiment and the fine line between the protection of US national interests and an act of war against the Nazis.

Through an exchange of letters and messages, the two leaders had developed a mutual admiration. Both were personally and politically tied to their navies, Churchill as previously First Lord of the Admiralty and Roosevelt as former Assistant Secretary of the US Navy. Each was cordial and affable, but above all there was an understanding that Britain had to prevail in the fight against Hitler and the Nazis. For Britain, victory meant survival. For the United States, the UK was the bulwark, its best defence against a burgeoning enemy that threatened to dominate Europe and perhaps the world.

By the summer of 1941, it seemed that exchanging messages had served its purpose. A face-to-face meeting – president and prime minister and their close advisors – was necessary. Arrangements were made amid tight security, and the leaders met on 9-12 August at Argentia on Placentia Bay along the coast of Canadian Newfoundland. The secluded area was perfect for the rendezvous, away from the press and the prying eyes of enemy agents. There was much to discuss: Britain had been fighting for two years but America remained officially neutral, although that status would come to an abrupt end four months later with the Japanese attack on Pearl Harbor on 7 December 1941.

In the meantime, the United States had become, in Roosevelt's words, "the great arsenal of democracy", sending massive amounts of supplies and war materiel to Britain across the Atlantic despite the efforts of Nazi U-boats to sever this lifeline. When Churchill had pleaded for old, First World War-vintage America destroyers to bolster the hard-pressed Royal Navy, Roosevelt responded with the 'Destroyers for Bases Deal' in September 1940. In the spring of 1941, the president managed to get Congressional approval for the Lend-Lease programme, allowing cash-strapped Britain to receive massive quantities of supplies and weapons without violating the US Neutrality Acts and bringing the US into the war.

In addition to this, the US Navy had begun limited escort duty of convoys in the Atlantic Ocean, engaging in a de facto shooting war with the Nazi U-boats that stalked the vital convoys. And just a month before the meeting at Placentia Bay the US sent troops to occupy Iceland, allowing the British to transfer military assets to other vital areas.

On 3 August 1941, Roosevelt departed Washington, DC, aboard the presidential yacht Potomac with the cover story that he intended to enjoy a few days of fishing. While a Secret Service

THE ATLANTIC CONFERENCE

THE END OF THE BEGINNING
1941-42

After the 'darkest hour' was over and an imminent invasion of Britain halted, the Allies nonetheless continued to be pushed back on nearly every front. With a first major battlefield success over the Axis proving elusive, Prime Minister Winston Churchill appealed to the United States to enter the war. By the end of 1942, the Allies not only counted the USA in their number but also the Soviet Union, with a string of victories inexorably turning the tide of the conflict.

agent stood in, waving to crowds along the Cape Cod Canal, the president had secretly transferred to the heavy cruiser USS Augusta for the historic meeting. Churchill crossed the Atlantic aboard the battleship HMS Prince of Wales. The two ships made rendezvous on 9 August, and much of the proceedings were held aboard Augusta due to Roosevelt's mobility challenges.

On Sunday 10 August, the leaders, their staffs and much of the ships' companies attended church services on the fantail of Prince of Wales. Churchill personally helped handle the rope as the destroyer USS McDougal tied up alongside the British battleship. He also chose the hymns that were sung, including Onward Christian Soldiers.

Although neither leader achieved everything that they desired with the Atlantic Conference, an understanding was reached. Among other issues, Churchill was disappointed with Roosevelt's refusal to discuss actual American entry into the war and his reluctance to warn Imperial Japan against territorial expansion in Asia and the Pacific. Meanwhile Roosevelt had hoped for a relaxation of Imperial Preference tariff restrictions and assurances of some framework for repayment of war debts. Nevertheless, the diplomatic alliance between the United States and Great Britain was affirmed, and the groundwork for the coming military alliance was firmly laid.

The most significant result of the Atlantic Conference was the issuance of a joint manifesto that came to be known as the Atlantic Charter, which clearly stated the common purpose of the future wartime allies, binding the nations together even more closely. The charter declared that neither nation sought any "aggrandizement, territorial or other" as a result of the war. It noted an agreement that no territorial realignment should occur without the consent of the people concerned and that those peoples deprived of self-government should have it restored with the right of self-determination. All nations, it related, should enjoy the right to trade freely across the open seas and to gain access to raw materials through cooperation. Finally, it asserted that with the destruction of Nazi Germany a lasting peace should be established, with the abandonment of war as a means of resolving international conflict.

Some historians point to the Atlantic Charter as the basis for the formation of the United Nations in 1945. While the British were somewhat troubled with the language of self-determination as they sought to maintain their empire amid a changing circumstance, Churchill urged Parliament to accept the charter without objection. Unnecessary difficulties, he said, would be "imprudent". Roosevelt succeeded in advancing principles of disarmament, free trade and self-determination in the postwar world. Overall, the issuance of the Atlantic Charter can be seen as the beginning of the end for Nazi Germany and the Axis powers: the US and Great Britain had demonstrated their high resolve and commitment to the defeat of tyranny

★ **KEY BATTLE** ★

SECOND BATTLE OF EL ALAMEIN

The First major Allied victory came when 8th Army launched a decisive offensive against the Axis forces in North Africa. It saw the tipping point of a long struggle for dominance over the region and precipitated the Axis collapse in the Mediterranean

WORDS **JOHN SADLER**

Hitler did not want to fight for North Africa in 1941, his eyes were staring eastwards towards steppe not the desert. Egypt was the prize his ally Benito Mussolini coveted. Yet Il Duce's ill-judged invasion of Greece was compounded by failure in Libya when Generals Wavell and O'Connor's strike in December 1940, Operation Compass, heralded disaster for Italy. Erwin Rommel was sent in with meagre forces, and grudgingly, to stem the rot. But this tortoise turned into a hare. The Desert Fox – generally at odds with his hosts and nominal superiors, not to mention High Command, was a maverick genius who began to rapidly turn the tide. It kept turning. The pendulum of war in the Western Desert began to swing, and it swung back and forth through abortive British offensives, Brevity and Battleaxe, then more tellingly with Claude Auchinleck's Crusader offensive.

But Rommel wasn't daunted. He struck back, harrying the Allies eastwards, past Gazala and Mersa Matruh, into Egypt and the El Alamein Line. Auchinleck saw him off in the First Battle of El Alamein (1-27 July 1942) but failed to mount a successful counterstroke. By now Churchill, desperate for a convincing victory, had had enough of 'The Auk' and his mercurial Chief of Staff Eric Dorman-Smith. He appointed General Harold Alexander to overall command and gave 8th Army, firstly to William Gott, whose death in a plane crash then cleared the path for Bernard Montgomery.

Monty was the new broom, as described in the *Official History (Volume 3)*: "General Montgomery… set to work at once to inspire confidence and enthusiasm in his Army." He first fought Rommel to a standstill at Alam Halfa (30 August – 5 September 1942) but made no immediate moves to riposte. Caution prevailed, and his offensive when it came would be based on significant superiority in men and materiel. Rommel was being starved of resources partly by Hitler (already Operation Barbarossa was in difficulties) and partly by Ultra as Enigma

Above: Bayonets fixed, Allied soldiers attack an Axis position during the decisive battle

SECOND BATTLE OF EL ALAMEIN

As the Allies pressed their advantage, Rommel eventually ignored Hitler's order not to retreat

Thousands of demoralised Italian troops surrendered during the fierce battle

"THIS IS NOT THE END. IT IS NOT EVEN THE BEGINNING OF THE END. BUT IT IS, PERHAPS, THE END OF THE BEGINNING"

Winston Churchill

intelligence enabled the Royal Navy to target Italian supply convoys. New Allied tanks (for instance, M4 Shermans) and improved six-pounder A/T guns eroded previous Axis tactical weapons superiority.

Out of the chaos of earlier retreats, the forced abandonment and destruction of materiel, order was re-emerging. With communication lines short and a great quantity of supplies flooding into Suez, losses were being made good. From Alamein to the main depot at El Amiriya was a barely 100km and links between there and Suez were functioning. Wavell's realisation that Egypt could be grown as a vast workhorse had, by 1942, become a tangible reality. The Nile Delta was a thriving war-based economy. Food was grown and reared, combining with a sophisticated industrial expansion aimed at maximum war production. These vital functions, undertaken respectively by the Royal Army Service Corps (RASC) and Royal Army Ordnance Corps (RAOC), provided Monty with the sinews of war in the desert.

As the autumn drew on the moment of decision grew nearer. This battle would be akin to a Great War 'break-in' offensive with the Allies chewing their way through deep Axis defences and sucking their reserves into a cauldron where sheer numbers would decide. But mere might, however crushing, can always use a helping hand.

Deception – Operation Bertram

As Montgomery described in his memoir, titled *Montgomery of Alamein*, the object of the deception plan was first to conceal from the enemy as long as possible our intention to take the offensive. When this could no longer be concealed, the aim was to mislead the enemy about both the date and the sector in which our main thrust was to be made.

Deceit in war is as old as conflict itself: from the Trojan Horse to Operation Fortitude which sought to confuse the Axis as to Allied intentions during the build-up to D-Day in the spring of 1944. In the case of Operation Lightfoot, as the break-in phase of the planned battle was called, deception was a significant part of overall preparation. In the north, 30 Corps sector, where the main attack was planned, a great mass of dummy vehicles, tanks and guns had been fabricated to create an impression of density. Immediately prior to the attack, under cover of darkness, these were replaced by the real thing and dummies transported to the rear. In this way, the static fiction was maintained. At the same time, Lt-Col Charles Richardson, 8th Army wizard masterminding the whole show, had to conceal vast supply dumps being created. That they were satisfactorily kept hidden was a masterpiece of disguise brought into being by Lieutenant-Colonel Geoffrey Barkas, director of Camouflage at GHQ Middle East.

Dumps, such as that at Imayid, covered very large areas, in this case some eight square kilometres. Dummy vehicles were again employed to conceal the crates of ammunition within the timber and canvas frames, and fuel cans were hidden in existing yet ostensibly abandoned trench lines. The distinctive 25-pounders, with their equally recognisable quad tractors to be concealed in the forward areas, were artfully disguised by fixing a false section to the tractor to make it resemble an ordinary truck, and by bunching gun and limber then placing a fake screen over the top.

"We were engaged in 'creating' a concourse of tanks and lorries and even an HQ to confuse the enemy reconnaissance planes," recalled one soldier in Alamein: Recollections of the Heroes. "It was all done by hessian, some string and some very light wood, poles etc. The dummy camp and vehicle sites were erected at night with the help of moonlight and during daylight gave the appearance of busy military areas to very high-flying enemy planes. Vehicles travelled around and about creating clouds of dust and in early morning every encouragement to brewing up among the dummy bivouac was given, and of course, round the vehicles, or tanks, outlined in hessian, supported by thin wooden poles or 'cats' cradles of strong twine."

To provide an impression that the main effort was to be directed toward the southern sector, part of the deception involved the construction of 30km of dummy 'Diamond' water pipeline. "The pipe-trench was excavated in the normal way," explained Montgomery in Montgomery of Alamein. "Five miles [8km] of dummy railway track, made from petrol cans, were used for piping. The 'piping' was strung out along the open trench. When each five-mile section of the trench was filled in, the 'piping' was collected and laid out alongside the next section. Dummy pump houses were erected at three points; water points and overhead storage reservoirs were made at two of these points."

He deemed Bertram a success but this is hard to evaluate. Nonetheless, Axis intelligence remained convinced the main blow must fall in the south. One vital area, wherein 8th Army's performance improved exponentially, was that of signals and wireless communication. Ultra intercepts betrayed every Axis move and Rommel's ears had been clipped with the elimination of his elite interceptors. 'Ghost' radio traffic was added to the web of deception to mask troop movements.

Troops of the 8th Army manning an artillery piece come under fire from enemy shells

One veteran recalled how they advanced accompanied by the "sort of orchestral music of the continuous guns in the background"

Operation Braganza

On the night of 29 September Lieutenant-General Brian Horrocks commanding 13 Corps to the south launched a preliminary mini-offensive. His objective was to seize ground by Deir el Munassib which would facilitate wider deployment of Allied guns prior to the main push.

One infantry brigade, 131st (Queens), together with elements from 4th Armoured supported by nine field artillery regiments and one medium battery, made up the contingent. Battle began at 05:25 hours when 1/6 Battalion, Queen's Royal Regiment (West Surrey) struck the northern shoulder with 1/7 battalion hitting the east. Opposition was relatively weak but 1/5 Battalion ran into tough Italian paras from 185th 'Folgore' Division when they attacked south. Overall, gains were meagre.

Horrocks tried a second push to capitalise on these limited successes, especially in the north where 132nd (Kent) Brigade made further gains. Ironically, more casualties resulted from heatstroke rather than wounds. In the south the British still managed little headway and Horrocks called off the attack.

Operation Lightfoot

Lieutenant-General Oliver Leese with 30 Corps would be responsible for the main effort in the north, where infantry would punch two corridors through Axis defences along which General Herbert Lumsden could send 10 Corps armour. The intention was that Allied tanks would pour through the gaps and draw Rommel's panzers into a melee, where they could be irretrievably ground down.

"THE DESERT RATS WERE NOT TO GET DRAWN INTO ATTRITIONAL 'DOGFIGHTS', THEY WERE TO HUSBAND THEIR STRENGTH"

Horrocks, in the southern sector with 13 Corps, would attack the enemy positions and operate with 7th Armoured Division to draw German armour in that direction. The aim was to make it easier for 10 Corps to break into the open to the north. The Desert Rats were not to get drawn into attritional 'dogfights', they were to husband their strength for pursuit once the breakout was achieved. Monty allowed himself full credit for the idea of delivering the main blow in the north and avoiding the tried tactic of a flanking attack from the south: "I planned to attack neither on my left flank nor on my right flank, but somewhere right of centre; having broken in, I could then direct my forces to the right or to the left as seemed most profitable."

Leese was to put four divisions into the attack. Nearest the coast the 9th Australian would have the extreme right, breaking in eastwards from Tel el Eisa. Next, the 51st Highland division was charged with assaulting towards Kidney Ridge. Then the 2nd New Zealand Division would strike towards the western extremity of Miteiriya Ridge with, on the far left, the 1st South African Division attacking the centre. The front stretched for 7km with a depth, on the right, of 8km shrinking to 4km on the left. Horrocks was to launch his offensive, diversions aside, on a narrower front with the 7th Armoured and 44th Division striking out south of Ruweisat Ridge.

In the main this was to convince the Axis forces that the main blow was falling in the south and to fix 21st Panzer's attention. Secondary objectives included attacks on Himeimat and Taqa Plateau, but these were not to be pressed home in the face of strong opposition. An intense artillery barrage would begin the fight at 21:40 on 23 October.

The guns would deluge German artillery with a weight of counter-battery fire before moving to plaster the forward defences. A rolling barrage would shield the attacking infantry battalions, proceeding in 'lifts'. With a sufficiency of anti-tank guns in theatre, the whole weight of field artillery could be brought to bear under a centralised fire plan.

As ever, the troops saw things in a rather more personal light: "We set off. Excited, breathless. And that sort of orchestral music of the continuous guns in the background," recalled one soldier. "We wondered if the Jerry saw it that way! I remember seeing a captain walking behind a Scorpion. Intent on supervising the job. This tank had a barrel fastened across its nose which revolved. Fastened by one end were chains which whirled round and thumped the ground ahead. Supposed to blow up any mines in its path. Something seemed to worry the captain and he literally screamed at the crew and someone nearby. On edge, poor devil. Some job!"

Below: *To deceive the Germans' observation planes, timber and canvas frames were used to disguise Allied artillery and tanks as trucks*

SECOND BATTLE OF EL ALAMEIN

Field Marshal Erwin Rommel (left) and General Ramcke pictured before the Second Battle of El Alamein

Operation Lightfoot saw Allied tanks pour through gaps in the Axis defences created by the infantry

Another man recounted: "So we set off late one evening, two battalions, two companies up in line abreast across a thousand yards of minefields, led by an officer on a compass bearing and Lieutenant-Colonel East using a stick as a result of a First World War wound. We were to advance behind a barrage of a thousand guns. There were casualties in the platoon on my right from one gun firing short or possibly from the enemy replying.

"I can still remember the shriek from one of my platoon when a booby trap on the barbed wire literally blew him to pieces… Eventually our leading platoon and the 1st /6th Queens on our left arrived in the middle of the Italian positions and some 20 to 30 Italians cheerfully gave themselves up and remained for the next 24 hours, withdrawing with us at the end of that time. The remainder of the Folgore Division, however, were made of sterner stuff and proceeded to inflict heavy casualties on us, using mortars and machine guns, firing from entrenched positions. I remember young O'Connell, both legs severed by a mortar bomb, screaming for help and then for his mother before he mercifully died."

Operation Supercharge

After the initial sound and fury of Lightfoot, followed by a period of attritional dogfighting ("crumbling", as Monty called it) there was still no sign of a breakthrough. Rommel was stretched but not bursting. It is impossible to overstate the advantages that accrued to the Allies through control of the skies and the havoc wrought by Desert Air Force. Though armoured formations were mostly safe, movement of soft-skinned Axis vehicles during this critical 'dogfight' phase was continually interdicted by attack from the air.

Nor should the corrosive effect on morale be overlooked, as Montgomery himself observed: "The morale effect of air action is very great and out of all proportion to the material damage inflicted. In reverse direction, the sight and sound of our own air forces operating against the enemy have an equally satisfactory effect on our own troops."

The Allies were winning the battle of attrition, but there was no great victory yet. As 8 November, the date fixed for the Operation Torch landings approached, Churchill needed a decision in the Western Desert.

"It was fairly clear to me that there had been consternation in Whitehall when I began to draw divisions into reserve on the 27th and 28th October, when I was getting ready for the final blow," said Montgomery. "Casey had been sent up to find out what was going on: Whitehall thought I was giving up, when in point of fact I was just about to win… I told him all about my plans and that I was certain of success; and de Guingand spoke to him very bluntly and told him to tell Whitehall not to bellyache. I never heard what signal was sent to London after the visit and was too busy to bother about it. Anyway, I was certain the CIGS [Chief of the Imperial General Staff]would know what I was up to."

Montgomery then went on to assess the tactical position at El Alamein and how he planned to launch his next major assault: "I decided on the night of 30/31 October the 9th Australian Division would attack strongly northwards to reach the sea; this would keep the enemy looking northwards.

"Then on the next night, 31 October/1 November, I would blow a deep hole in the enemy front just to the north of the original corridor; this hole would be made by 2nd New Zealand Division which would be reinforced by the 9th Armoured brigade and two infantry brigades; the operation would be under the command of 30 Corps.

"Through the gap I would pass 10 Corps with its armoured divisions… We already had the necessary divisions in reserve, and they had been resting and refitting… What in fact, I proposed to do was to deliver a hard blow with the right and follow it the next night with a knock-out blow with the left!"

This decisive phase, codenamed SUPERCHARGE, lasted from 29 October to 4 November and continued the process of attrition. Monty was aided by Hitler, who issued an order that no foot of ground should be yielded. Wisely, Rommel eventually ignored him. Monty switched his main drive to the north and gradually the weight of attacks fractured the Axis lines. This time the rupture was fatal.

Assessments differ, but the Axis had lost around 30,000 prisoners, two-thirds Italian, and perhaps as many as 20,000 dead and wounded. Most of his Italian formations had been decimated and such transport as could be found reserved for German survivors. Out of nearly 250 tanks they could barely field three dozen. It was not just the end of the beginning but for Nazi Germany the beginning of the end.

KEY BATTLE

MIDWAY

TURNING POINT OF THE PACIFIC WAR

Just six months after Pearl Harbor, Japan launched another attack on the US Navy. James Holland explains how this time the US was prepared and the resulting clash turned the tide of the war

WORDS **NICK SOLDINGER**

Douglas SBD-2 Dauntless dive bombers on the USS Enterprise prepare for an attack on Japanese ships during the Battle of Midway

MIDWAY

A Douglas SBD-2 Dauntless on the USS Hornet. The type played a pivotal role in the US victory

By 1942, the war appeared to be going well for Japan. Since December 1941, it had conquered a series of territories throughout Asia and the Pacific. In quick succession, it had seized Hong Kong and Malaya from the British, overrun large parts of the Dutch East Indies and had chased the Americans out of the Philippines. In doing so, it had plundered many of the resources it would need to continue the expansion of its empire. However, one major obstacle still needed to be overcome before victory.

Yamamoto's plan

Midway Atoll is a 2.3 square-mile (six-square-kilometre) scrap of volcanic land marooned in the vast blue of the Pacific Ocean. Consisting largely of two tiny, flat islands called Sand and Eastern, it lies 1,073 miles (1,728 kilometres) west of Pearl Harbor, roughly halfway between San Francisco and Tokyo. In 1939, it was one of the most western US outposts.

This made it vital both as a defensive asset for the US West Coast and as a staging post for Allied ships and aircraft headed into the Pacific theatre. Yamamoto planned to seize Midway in a surprise attack that would take place in three phases. First, his carrier fleet, known as Kido Butai, under Admiral Chuichi Nagumo, would attack Midway by air with aircraft from its four powerful flattops: Soryu, Hiryu, Kaga and its flagship Akagi. Once Midway's defences were destroyed, a 5,000-strong invasion force would then be brought in by a second fleet of ships commanded by Vice Admiral Nobutake Kondo. Expecting the US to then send everything it could to repel the invaders, Yamamoto's total force of around 200 warships would then converge on Midway from across the Pacific to crush what was left of the US Pacific Fleet.

Yamamoto expected his plan to deliver a decisive victory for Japan and establish another foothold in the Pacific, finally forcing America into submission. It was an audacious gamble by the Japanese.

US codebreakers and Midway

In March 1942, a team of cryptographers led by Captain Joseph Rochefort had largely broken the secret code used by the Japanese Navy in its radio transmissions. For months they had been monitoring and deciphering every message they'd intercepted and were fully aware the enemy was planning an attack.

The main objective, however, remained a mystery as it was only ever referred to by the Japanese as 'AF'. On 20 May, Rochefort's team sent out a fake dispatch about water shortages on Midway. As hoped, it was picked up by Tokyo Naval Intelligence who forwarded it on, declaring 'AF' to be short of water. In doing so, they confirmed Midway as the intended target. Rochefort immediately reported what he'd discovered to Admiral Chester Nimitz, commander-in-chief of the US Pacific Fleet, who started drawing up his own plan.

When the Japanese attacked, Nimitz decided he would engage them mainly from the air, keeping the three carriers he had available split into two groups and well out of striking distance of the Japanese ships.

The first group, Task Force 17, was led by Admiral Frank Jack Fletcher and consisted of two cruisers and the carrier USS Yorktown. The second group, Task Force 16, was led by Rear Admiral Raymond Spruance and included the aircraft carriers Enterprise and Hornet, accompanied by six cruisers.

By the beginning of June, Nimitz's trap was set. Rather than being holed up in Pearl Harbor as the Japanese believed, his aircraft carriers were lying in wait 348 miles (560km) north of Midway with the Kido Butai steaming towards them.

Dawn, 4 June 1942

The Kido Butai carrier fleet, commanded by Admiral Nagumo, is approximately 149 miles (240km) northwest of Midway, and is forming the spearhead of the Japanese attack. Yamamoto splits his force into several fleets and scatters them across the Pacific. The day before, a US patrol plane sighted Kondo's invasion force 497 miles (800km) south of Midway, while Yamamoto was with the main force a further 600 miles (965km) to the west. His reason for doing this was to both avoid detection as well as appear under-strength.

According to Holland, however, this created two big problems for him: "First, the various fleets can't communicate except by radio, which means any message they send runs the risk of being intercepted and decrypted. Secondly, by trying to mask what he's up to by keeping his full force so spread out, his ships are too far apart to be mutually supportive. It's a massive blunder."

4:30am

Nagumo orders the airstrike against Midway to begin. Within ten minutes, 108 aircraft, including A6M 'Zero' fighters, D3A 'Val' dive bombers and B5N 'Kate' torpedo-bombers have swarmed into the air and are headed towards the atoll.

At around the same time, the Americans, aware of what is coming, launch their own attacks. Taking off from Midway, a force of over 50 bombers, including Grumman TBF Avengers, Martin B-26 Marauders, Douglas SBD-2 Dauntlesses, Vought SB2U Vindicators and B-17 Flying Fortresses sets off to attack the Japanese carriers.

5:56am

The haunting wail of Midway's air-raid siren announces the incoming Japanese planes. The base's fighters scramble. Six Grumman F4 Wildcats and 20 Brewster F2A Buffalos engage the Japanese, only to suffer devastating losses. Heavily outnumbered by the more agile Zeros, two Wildcats and 13 Buffalos are shot down.

6:16am

The Japanese bombers now hit both Eastern and Sand Island. Various facilities including oil tanks, the power plant, a seaplane hangar, the mess hall and the hospital are all hit. Of the 108 Japanese planes involved in the attack, 11 are destroyed and a further 14 are badly damaged, largely by ground fire. Crucially, however, they fail to inflict significant damage on the base's runway.

Nagumo's dilemma at Midway

7:05am

The raid's leader breaks radio silence to inform Nagumo that another air raid is needed to destroy the base's defences if a successful invasion is to take place. Having kept back roughly half of his planes in case of contact with the US carriers, Nagumo is now faced with a difficult decision. Does he send in

> "YAMAMOTO KNEW THAT A DECISIVE HAMMER BLOW STILL NEEDED TO BE DEALT AGAINST THE US AND IT NEEDED TO BE DEALT QUICKLY"

a second wave of aircraft to finish off Midway or does he hold them back as ordered?

As he gives the order for his reserve aircraft to be prepared for a second air raid, the US bomber force from Midway appears overhead and begins to attack his ships. It's the first indication that the Americans must have known about the attack and have prepared a trap; more evidence soon presents itself when Nagumo receives a report from a Japanese spotter plane that ten US warships are lurking in waters 240 miles (386km) north of Midway. He asks if any carriers are among them and waits for confirmation.

8:20am
With US planes continuing to attack his carriers, Nagumo finally receives the news he's been dreading the most – there is at least one carrier among the US ships north of Midway. The Admiral desperately needs to launch an attack against this force immediately to halt the threat, but unfortunately he has ordered his reserve planes to be fitted with ordinance to hit land targets at Midway.

Reversing this order they are now rearmed for a naval engagement, but the clock is ticking. The 97 planes from the initial raid on Midway are due to return at any minute. They will be low on fuel and if his flight decks aren't clear will have to ditch into the sea. He delays his strike.

Five minutes that change history
9:15am
Just as the last of Nagumo's planes are returning from the Midway raid, a force of 15 US Devastator dive bombers is spotted closing in on his fleet. They are the first of more than 100 aircraft launched from the US carriers to attack the Japanese.

Unescorted by fighters, all 15 are quickly shot down without inflicting any damage. As soon as this attack is over another one begins. This time, a force of 14 Devastators attack, again with heavy losses and no hits. Not long after, a third wave of planes appears. Made up of 12 Devastators and six Wildcats, this attack is also a complete failure as they're picked apart by Zeros.

10:22am
Seventeen Dauntless dive bombers now approach from the north while another 31 fly in from the south. Undetected and unopposed, a group of 30 dive on the Kaga from 19,000 feet, scoring four direct hits, one of which destroys the bridge and kills the captain.

Fires rage below decks and the fully fuelled and armed planes waiting in the hangars catch alight, causing a wave of secondary explosions to sweep through the ship. A force of 13 dive bombers now attacks the Soryu, hitting her flight deck three times and causing a chain of explosions to rip through her hangars. Just

SBD Dauntless dive bombers fly over a burning Japanese ship during the attack off Midway

An American oil storage facility on Midway is destroyed by Japanese aircraft

Flak bursts above the stricken carrier USS Yorktown, already hit by enemy bombardment

"JUST AS THE LAST OF NAGUMO'S PLANES ARE RETURNING FROM THE MIDWAY RAID, A FORCE OF 15 US DEVASTATOR DIVE BOMBERS IS SPOTTED CLOSING IN ON HIS FLEET"

like the Kaga, she too is soon a raging inferno. Three bombers that had been headed for the Kaga now switch targets and go after the Akagi.

A bomb strikes a fully laden plane waiting on her deck and a chain of explosions now tears through Nogumo's flagship. Japan's carriers have been all but wiped out – only the Hiryu remains intact. "At 10.21am the Americans had been losing the battle, by 10.27am they're not only winning it, they're winning the war. It's arguably the most decisive few minutes in the history of the Second World War," says Holland.

The Japanese counterattack
11:00am
Having left his blazing flagship to the light cruiser Nagara, Nagumo finally orders the attack against the US ships that the constant American attacks have prevented him from launching. Eighteen Val dive bombers with an escort of six Zero fighters take off from the Hiryu. En route, they encounter a group of six Dauntless dive bombers returning to their carriers. The Zeros peel off to engage.

A short exchange follows and although no aircraft are lost on either side, the skirmish leaves two Zeros so damaged they have to return to the Hiryu. This unnecessary action also leaves the Val bombers without protection as the four remaining Zeros now desperately try to catch up with them as they close in.

11:52am
USS Yorktown's radar picks up the incoming Val bomber group and 20 Wildcat fighters are scrambled to engage it. With its reduced fighter escort still lagging behind, the Wildcats rip through the heavier, more clumsy bombers. Seven are shot down before the Zeros can reach them and then, in the dogfight that follows, a further four Vals and three Zeros are lost for the cost of one Wildcat. There are now just seven Vals left to carry out the attack on the Yorktown. Splitting into two groups, three bombers now race towards the ship from the west while the other four weave through the flak from the southwest.

12:00pm
The first Val is blown out of the sky, but not before it manages to score a direct hit on the Yorktown. Another Val is also lost, but in all the Japanese manage a further two hits on the US carrier, setting it ablaze and bringing it to a halt.

With the ship out of action, Admiral Fletcher transfers to the heavy cruiser USS Astoria and hands over his command of the battle to Rear Admiral Spruance on the USS Enterprise.

1:30pm
A second strike force made up of ten Kate torpedo bombers escorted by six Zero fighters takes off from the Hiryu to attack the US carriers. An hour later, its pilots also encounter the Yorktown. Six Wildcats engage the group, shooting down a single Kate.

The rest of the torpedo bombers, however, get through. Skimming over the water through a blizzard of anti-aircraft fire, they split into two groups to attack the stricken ship from both sides. The four planes approaching from starboard are all downed without scoring a single hit. The five attacking from port side, however, strike the carrier twice. A huge hole is punched into its hull that leaves it listing so badly its deck is almost touching the water.

3:00pm
The order is given to abandon ship to prevent further loss of life, although it will take until the morning of 7 June for Yorktown to eventually sink. With the Hiryu now only 71 miles (115km) out from the other two US carriers, Spruance orders all available dive bombers to attack it. Forty unescorted Dauntless planes are dispatched from Enterprise and Hornet, leaving the fighters behind to defend the carriers.

4:45pm
The US bombers sight the Hiryu as Nagumo's fleet retreats west. Moving west to attack out of the sun, the Americans hope to surprise the Japanese for a second time that day.

"The fact that the Japanese didn't have radar at that stage of the war is really significant," explains Holland. "They've got all these incredibly technically advanced warships and aircraft carriers yet they're missing that vital piece of equipment and it costs them."

5:01pm
The Dauntlesses rain down bombs on the Hiryu and within five minutes have scored four direct hits. The explosions cause fires to rage through the hangars on the lower decks, again setting planes and munitions alight.

The fires are so intense that the remaining Dauntlesses peel off and attack the Hiryu's escort ships instead. Later that night, just before midnight, a huge explosion rips through the carrier and at 3.15am on 5 June the order is given to abandon ship.

Although there are further minor skirmishes over the next few days, the destruction of the Hiryu effectively brings the battle to a close.

Aftermath
It wasn't just the loss of the carriers of the Kido Butai that was to prove so devastating for the Japanese. "What's also significant is the loss of around 200 of their most experienced pilots," says Holland. "These men had been flying for years. They had 500 to 1,000 hours in their logbooks and were the absolute cream. They were irreplaceable. Japan could and did build other carriers but it never had the resources or the time to train subsequent pilots as well."

The defeat at Midway put the Japanese on the back foot for the rest of the war as the US now went on the offensive. Victory after victory followed for the Americans as they fought their way across the Pacific.

"It turned into this really brutal, attritional war with Japan desperately scrabbling about for resources," says Holland, "Midway really was the last throw of the dice for the Japanese and afterwards, as America threw its full industrial might into the conflict, there was just no way back for them. They still sank American carriers, cruisers and battleships, but it was never enough."

Although Japan had no hope of winning, it stubbornly refused to admit defeat. The war dragged on for the another three years with only atomic weapons bringing an end to its leaders' imperial ambitions.

KEY BATTLE

GUADALCANAL

Operation Watchtower, the first US land offensive during the Second World War, wrested the Pacific island from Japanese control

WORDS **MIKE HASKEW**

GUADALCANAL

By the summer of 1942, American and Allied forces in the Pacific Theatre of World War II were finally poised to assume the offensive. Operation Watchtower, the campaign to secure the southern Solomon Islands, was conceived to deter Japanese southward expansion. Enemy presence in the region could threaten tenuous supply and communication lines stretching from the West Coast of the United States to remote Pacific bases, and to Australia.

Early in 1942, Japanese troops began constructing a seaplane base on the island of Tulagi and an airstrip at Lunga Point on Guadalcanal, 35 kilometres to the south across Sealark Channel. When these bases became operational, critical Allied installations would be within range of Japanese aircraft.

The only alternative for the Americans was to attack. Operation Watchtower, set for 7 August 1942, was designed to capture Guadalcanal, Tulagi, and the neighbouring islands of Tanambogo and Gavutu, and the task fell initially to the US 1st Marine Division, under General Alexander A Vandegrift. The division, 19,000 strong, was to receive logistical support from Task Force 61, under Admiral Frank Jack Fletcher, while amphibious forces under Admiral Richmond Kelly Turner put the fighting men ashore, 11,000 of them on Guadalcanal. Admiral Robert L Ghormley, commander of US forces in the South Pacific Area, was responsible for the overall effort.

When the Marines splashed ashore at Tulagi, Tanambogo and Gavutu, heavy fighting ensued, but the islands were secured within three days. At Guadalcanal, the Marines met virtually no resistance on the beaches. Surprisingly, they established a beachhead more than 1,800 metres long and 550 metres deep. On 8 August they secured the airfield.

It was the calm before the storm. During the next six months, fighting raged on Guadalcanal as well as the airspace and seas around the island. No fewer than seven naval battles, five of them nocturnal, took a heavy toll, earning Sealark Channel a new name – 'Iron Bottom Sound'. Fighting in fetid jungles and swamps, Marines and US Army troops captured Guadalcanal the following February. The cost was high with 1,600 killed and 4,200 wounded. Japanese losses were catastrophic with more than 24,000 dead.

As soon as the Americans had taken the airstrip, they renamed it Henderson Field in honour of a Marine pilot killed in the recent Battle of Midway. Navy construction battalions (Seabees) completed the airstrip, making it operational for US planes. Control of Henderson Field became the linchpin of victory at Guadalcanal. The landings had taken the Japanese by surprise. Rather than launching an overwhelming counterattack on land, their response ashore was piecemeal, although air attacks and naval sorties threatened to thwart Operation Watchtower.

On the night of 8 August a Japanese naval task force sank the US cruisers Astoria, Vincennes and Quincy, and the Australian cruiser Canberra in the Battle of Savo Island. Fletcher began withdrawing his fleet. Many ships still had their cargoes aboard, and the Marines were essentially marooned with only 17 days' rations with which to survive. They scrounged food, conserved water and fought like lions.

A concerted Japanese effort to eject the Americans from Guadalcanal was not undertaken until mid-August, when the 28th Infantry Regiment, under Colonel Kiyonao Ichiki, made landfall. The impetuous Ichiki struck at American positions along the Ilu River, misidentified on Marine maps as the Tenaru, on the night of 21 August. The 2nd Battalion, 1st Marines absorbed the brunt of the assault, and American light tanks, artillery, machine-gun and rifle fire shredded clusters of enemy troops attempting to cross the river. After daylight, the Marines mopped up. 800 Japanese soldiers were dead, while 34 Marines were killed and 75 wounded. Distraught, Ichiki burned his regimental standard and committed suicide. Henderson Field was safe, but only temporarily.

The Japanese continued to deliver supplies and reinforcements via nocturnal runs down New Georgia Sound, nicknamed 'The Slot', and these fast convoys were soon dubbed the 'Tokyo Express' by the Americans. Meanwhile,

A US Marine looking out over the scene of heavy fighting on Guadalcanal, November 1942

US fighters and bombers, dubbed the 'Cactus Air Force', engaged in dogfights with enemy planes, interdicted Japanese bombing missions and strafed targets of opportunity, including enemy troop transports caught during daylight hours. Marine Major Joseph J Foss led the fighter pilots, becoming an ace and shooting down 23 Japanese aircraft in October and November. Still, the American grip on Henderson Field remained tenuous, and the Japanese were full of fight.

Marine Raiders and airborne troops moved from Tulagi to Guadalcanal in September, joining the 2nd Battalion, 5th Marines defending a line facing west to protect Henderson Field. An all-out Japanese effort to break through and take the airfield was launched after dark on 12 September. Lieutenant Colonel Merritt A 'Red Mike' Edson led a desperate Marine defence against multiple enemy charges.

In some places, fighting was hand-to-hand. Marine artillery was on time and accurate, blasting the Japanese, whose attacking waves finally receded. Afterwards, the area of sharpest fighting bore the name of 'Bloody Ridge' or 'Edson's Ridge' after the gallant commander. More than 800 Japanese troops died, and around 600 were wounded. Marine losses amounted to 59 killed and 200 wounded.

At sea, the struggle swirled. On 24 to 25 August, the Battle of the Eastern Solomons was fought to a bloody draw with the aircraft carrier USS Enterprise damaged. In early October, the Japanese landed reinforcements despite American interference during the nocturnal Battle of Cape Esperance.

In the Battle of the Santa Cruz Islands on 25 to 26 October, the aircraft carrier Hornet was lost, while Enterprise was damaged once again, but two Japanese carriers were damaged and their aircrews suffered terrible losses. In mid-November, a Japanese reinforcement mission was stopped during the Naval Battle of Guadalcanal, but on the 15th the aircraft carrier USS Wasp was torpedoed and sunk by a Japanese submarine. At the end of the month, the Japanese won a tactical victory at the Battle of Tassafaronga but again failed to put troops and supplies ashore on the island.

Unable to establish complete control of the sea or air around Guadalcanal, Japanese senior commanders realised that their ability to contest the island was slipping away. They also understood that the fight had taken on a much greater significance than they had originally assigned it. In one last gamble for victory, they committed two full divisions to battle.

General Harukichi Hyakutake arrived on the island in early October, and a week later the Marines received reinforcements from the 23rd (Americal) Division of the US Army. Admiral Robert L Ghormley was relieved on 18 October, replaced with Admiral William F 'Bull' Halsey, a tough-minded commander intent on winning. Hyakutake continued his troop buildup and then hurled thousands against the 1st Battalion, 7th Marines, under Lieutenant Colonel Lewis B 'Chesty' Puller, reinforced by the 164th Infantry Regiment, Americal Division, along the Matanikau River on 24 to 25 October. The Americans were hard-pressed. One battalion endured three fanatical Japanese charges on the second day, but the offensive blew itself out, gaining nothing at a cost of 3,500 dead. American casualties amounted to 300 killed and wounded.

In November, the Americans began clearing pockets of resistance along the Matanikau while holding their line against repeated enemy attacks. In December, the 1st Marine Division was finally withdrawn after four months in combat. Army Lieutenant General Alexander M Patch relieved the heroic Vandegrift, and his new command of 50,000 troops included the 2nd Marine Division, and the Army's Americal and 25th Infantry Divisions. At the end of the month, Patch initiated a decisive push. Enemy resistance began to noticeably wane by the

US 1st Marine Division storm the beaches of Guadalcanal on 7 August 1942

US Marines rest in a jungle clearing on Guadalcanal during operations against the defending Japanese forces

- **7 AUGUST 1942**
  OPERATION WATCHTOWER UNDERWAY
  1st Marine Division storm Guadalcanal against the Japanese opposition.

- **8 AUGUST 1942**
  DISASTER AT SAVO ISLAND
  Japanese gunnery and torpedo tactics sink four Allied cruisers, prompting Admiral Fletcher to withdraw American naval forces off Guadalcanal.

- **21 AUGUST 1942**
  ICHIKI DETACHMENT DECIMATED
  Marines along the Tenaru (Ilu) River annihilate the Japanese 28th Infantry Regiment, under Colonel Kiyonao Ichiki, as they vainly attempt to cross the stream and capture vital Henderson Field.

- **24 AUGUST 1942**
  EASTERN SOLOMONS BATTLE
  In the naval Battle of the Eastern Solomons, both sides suffer losses to air attacks.

- **12 SEPTEMBER 1942**
  BATTLE OF BLOODY RIDGE
  Marines under Lieutenant Colonel Merritt A 'Red Mike' Edson defend Henderson Field on Guadalcanal.

- **24 SEPTEMBER 1942**
  AMERICAN FIGHTERS PROWL
  The Cactus Air Force, based at Henderson Field, shoot down 16 enemy aircraft. Marine Captain Marion E Carl claims three.

GUADALCANAL

US Marines landing on Guadalcanal ahead of the gruelling six-month campaign

end of January, and on 9 February 1943, Guadalcanal was declared secure.

The Japanese had sustained mounting losses in their reinforcement efforts and concluded that the necessary pace would be unsustainable. Many soldiers were suffering from disease and malnutrition. In mid-December, Imperial General Headquarters had decided to abandon the island, finally evacuating about 11,000 emaciated soldiers.

With the victories at Midway and Guadalcanal, the Americans seized the initiative in the Pacific War and began the long, bloody campaign on the island road to Tokyo. US strategic planners had identified two specific operational areas in the Pacific. General Douglas MacArthur, Commander-in-Chief South West Pacific, was to lead an offensive through the Solomons, New Guinea, the Bismarck Islands and the Philippines, while Admiral Chester W Nimitz, Supreme Commander Pacific Ocean Areas, would conduct a series of amphibious operations against Japanese-held islands in the Gilbert, Marshall and Marianas archipelagos. This two-pronged offensive would stretch the Japanese capacity to wage defensive war to its limits.

The Americans intended to prosecute their offensive across the Pacific, bypassing some enemy-occupied islands identified during tactical assessment and severing their critical supply lines. US military planners were confident that this island-hopping strategy would cause these bypassed and isolated Japanese strongholds to wither on the vine. In practice, the strategy proved quite effective.

"During the summer and autumn of 1943, American forces in the Pacific were strengthened with the introduction of the Essex-class aircraft carrier, the Iowa-class battleship and the Grumman F6F Hellcat fighter," historian John Wukovits explains. "These state-of-the-art weapons platforms were instrumental in waging the offensive war against Japan.

"In addition, the US Marine Corps and US Army committed growing numbers of fighting men to the effort. While MacArthur attacked in the Solomons and New Guinea, Nimitz launched the series of amphibious landings in the Central Pacific. The first of these occurred at Tarawa and Makin in the Gilberts in November 1943."

In 1944, the Americans wrested control of key island fortresses from the Japanese, including Kwajalein and Eniwetok in the Marshalls; and Guam, Saipan and Tinian in the Marianas. In June of that year, Japanese naval air power was virtually annihilated at the Battle of the Philippine Sea, and in October the IJN was again defeated in the decisive Battle of Leyte Gulf. This Japanese defeat coincided with MacArthur's forces landing in the Philippines on the island of Leyte, marking the general's much-publicised return.

- **11–12 OCTOBER 1942**
  BATTLE OF CAPE ESPERANCE
  Both sides lose a cruiser and a destroyer to naval gunfire.

- **18 OCTOBER 1942**
  HALSEY RELIEVES GHORMLEY
  Admiral Ghormley, believed too pessimistic to continue in overall command of Operation Watchtower, is relieved by Admiral William F 'Bull' Halsey, who energises the campaign.

- **24–25 OCTOBER 1942**
  CHESTY PULLER'S STAND
  Marine Lieutenant Colonel Lewis Puller exhorts his command, to stand firm against waves of attacking Japanese troops in a decisive engagement.

- **25–26 OCTOBER 1942**
  SANTA CRUZ ACTION
  The aircraft carrier USS Hornet sinks, while Enterprise is damaged. Supporting a Guadalcanal land offensive, the Japanese fail to control the seas, losing veteran aircrews.

- **25 DECEMBER 1942**
  PULLING THE PLUG
  Conceding that the battle for Guadalcanal is lost, senior Japanese officers gather at the Imperial Palace in Tokyo to finalise plans for troops withdrawal.

- **9 FEBRUARY 1943**
  FROM DOUBT TO VICTORY
  Operation Watchtower concludes as the island of Guadalcanal is pronounced secure by American forces.

Churchill, Harriman, Stalin and Molotov at the Moscow Conference

★ 12 AUGUST 1942 ★

THE MOSCOW CONFERENCE

Churchill's secret mission to Moscow forged an alliance between ideological adversaries that was crucial to the outcome of the war

WORDS **JOHN BEALES**

THE MOSCOW CONFERENCE

Despite decades of anti-communist rhetoric, after Germany's invasion of its erstwhile ally in 1941, Winston Churchill made speeches recognising the Russians as comrades-in-arms. He declared: "The Russian danger is therefore our danger, and the danger of the United States, just as the cause of any Russian fighting for his hearth and home is the cause of free men and free peoples in every quarter of the globe."

In the USSR things were going badly. For Joseph Stalin the pressing issue was the opening of a second front, and he had repeatedly advocated that Britain and the USA launch an invasion of occupied France. Churchill knew this was logistically impossible but wisely realised that such news was best delivered in person. In August 1942 he decided to meet Stalin face-to-face for the first time, to secure an alliance that would enable a co-ordinated campaign against Nazi Germany. He sent a telegram to Stalin proposing a meeting, stating: "We could survey the war together and take decisions hand-in-hand. I could then tell you plans we have made with President Roosevelt for offensive action in 1942."

Knowing that the Russian leader was notoriously paranoid and allegedly afraid of flying, Churchill's masterstroke was to agree to meet him in Moscow. Flying from RAF Lyneham, Churchill's arduous journey took him via Gibraltar, Cairo and Tehran, arriving in Moscow late on the afternoon of Wednesday 12 August 1942 accompanied by Sir Alec Cadogan of the Foreign Office and an American representative, Averell Harriman. Another aircraft carrying the remainder of the British delegation suffered technical problems and returned to Tehran. Despite the last leg of the journey taking just over 10 hours, early that evening Churchill had what would be a momentous first meeting with Stalin.

Its first few hours were tense and sombre. Stalin reported the Germans' continuing advances on the Eastern Front and pressed Churchill and Harriman about the opening of a second front. After they informed Stalin that it was impossible to amass the huge number of men and materiel needed for an invasion of Europe in 1942, Stalin angrily asked why they were so afraid of the Germans.

His mood was changed by Churchill's discussion of a planned mass bombing campaign of Germany, and an Anglo-American secret: their plans to invade Vichy French-controlled North Africa in November 1942, codenamed Operation Torch. This, Churchill argued, would enable a later invasion of Italy and open a new supply route to Russia via the Mediterranean and Black seas. After nearly four hours they parted amicably for the night. Churchill returned to his accommodation and reportedly remarked to one of his advisors that Stalin was a "peasant" whom he could handle. It's possible that the accommodation was bugged, because the next day tensions resurfaced.

Churchill appraised the Soviet Commissar for Foreign Affairs Vyacheslav Molotov of the build-up of American forces in Britain, plans for Operation Torch and the possibility of an Anglo-Soviet invasion of Norway. But it was not until very late that night, after the remainder of the British delegation had arrived, that a meeting was held with Stalin. It did not begin well.

Stalin again criticised the abandonment of plans for opening a second front in 1942 and the lack of aid supplied to the USSR, arguing that Operation Torch would have no impact on the conflict in Russia. "You British are afraid of fighting," he repeated. Cadogan later recorded that the day had been "as sticky and unhelpful as could be". Yet Churchill's and Harriman's reassurances to Stalin about Operation Torch and the Arctic convoys supplying Russia, combined with the spirit of Churchill's oratory, seemingly saved the day.

The following day they attended a banquet with nearly 100 guests, during which Stalin toasted Churchill, Harriman and President Roosevelt, followed by a private meeting with Stalin. Churchill travelled to the Kremlin again the next day and was invited for drinks at Stalin's private residence that night. It would turn into a relaxed and boozy meal with Stalin and his daughter. Early on 16 August, Stalin and Churchill released a statement that the Soviet Union, Great Britain and the USA would jointly fight until "Hitlerism" and similar "tyranny" had been defeated.

Churchill's development of a rapport with Stalin ultimately enabled him to act as broker between the USA and the USSR, and led to the formation of the Grand Alliance. By convincing Stalin that Operation Torch would be to Russia's benefit, and by agreeing to intensify the bombing campaign against Germany, as well as supplying more war materiel to Russia, he increased Stalin's confidence in the British and American strategy and the benefits of an alliance. Stalin also came to accept that Britain and the USA would decide the timetabling of the invasion of France.

KEY TECH

ILYUSHIN IL-2 SHTURMOVIK

The 'bread and air' of the Soviet Air Force during the Second World War

WORDS STUART HADAWAY

By 1944, the Ilyushin Il-2 Shturmovik made up around 30% of the Soviet Air Force's front line. This rugged and versatile aircraft packed a heavy punch that inflicted untold damage on the German invaders from June 1941 right through to the end of the war. It was one of the most successful ground attack aircraft ever built, and the term 'Shturmovik' went from being the generic Soviet designation for a ground attack aircraft to be being indelibly linked to this one type. Over 36,000 were made, and it is little wonder that the Soviet Army called the Shturmovik the 'Flying Tank', the German Army called it the 'Black Death', and Joseph Stalin called it the 'bread and air' of the Soviet Air Force.

The Il-2 was heavily armoured and armed, but easy to operate and maintain in rough field conditions. Optimised for low-level attack, it could both hand out and soak up heavy damage. Although early, single-seat models were vulnerable to German fighter attack, the most common variant (the two-seat Il-2m3) was brutally effective, capable of destroying not only Germany's heaviest tanks but also wreaking havoc among the transport that constantly struggled to keep their armies supplied.

Shturmoviks sweep in for an attack, November 1941

Over 36,000 Shturmoviks were built during WWII and the aircraft played a crucial role in driving the Nazis out of the USSR

ILYUSHIN IL-2M3

COMMISSIONED:	1938
ORIGIN:	SOVIET UNION
LENGTH:	11.6M (38FT 3IN)
WINGSPAN:	14.6M (47FT 11IN)
ENGINE:	MIKULIN AM38F 1,270KW (1,700HP) V-12 ENGINE
CREW:	2
PRIMARY WEAPON:	2 X 23MM VYA OR 37MM N37 CANNON, 2 X 7.62MM MACHINE GUNS, 1 X 12.7MM MACHINE GUN
SECONDARY WEAPON:	UP TO 600KG (1,323LB) BOMBS, ROCKETS, OR A 53CM TORPEDO

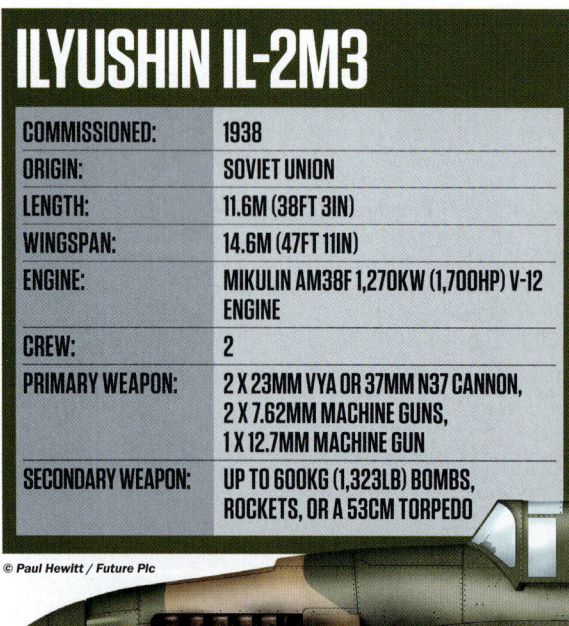

ILYUSHIN IL-2 SHTURMOVIK

> "THE ARMOURED FRONT WAS NEVER COMPROMISED AND GAVE THE AIRCRAFT (AND ESPECIALLY THE ENGINE AND CREW) SUPERB PROTECTION"

A formation of Shturmoviks on the hunt for enemy targets

ARMAMENT

The Il-2m3 had two cannon (23mm VYa, or from 1943 37mm N37) and two 7.62mm ShKAS machine guns fixed in the wings, operated by the pilot. A single 12.7mm Berezin UBT machine gun was operated by the rear gunner. Six 100kg (220lb) bombs or four PTAB anti-tank bomblet dispensers (totalling 192 bomblets) could be carried in small bomb bays in the wing roots and externally on pylons. Eight small RS82 or four larger RS132 rockets could also be carried on pylons, while the naval variant carried a 53cm torpedo.

An armourer reloads the cannon on an Il-2

A formation of Shturmoviks could inflict incredible damage to already fragile German supply lines

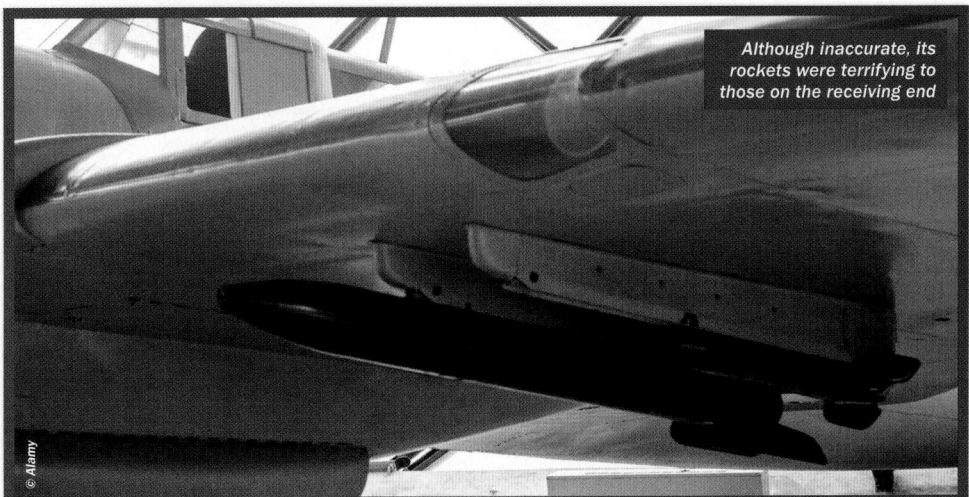

Although inaccurate, its rockets were terrifying to those on the receiving end

ENGINE

The Shturmovik was powered by a single Mikulin AM38 liquid-cooled V-12 engine, driving a three-bladed metal variable pitch propeller. The Il-2m3 used the AM38F, which was strengthened and improved for better performance on take-off. Although it had a higher fuel consumption than the earlier models, the AM38F gave the pilot smoother control and overall better efficiency. It was designed for low-level use in the Il-2 and later Il-10 ground attack aircraft, which seldom operated at an altitude of more than a few thousand metres.

The Shturmovik was heavy for a single-engine aircraft, but only operated at low altitudes

DESIGN

The Il-2's design centred around its armoured cockpit area. This steel 'bath' encompassed the engine, oil and fuel tanks, and both crew. Rather than adding armour to an airframe, this thick structure formed the entire forward section of the aircraft. Metal-framed and metal-skinned wings and rear structure were attached directly. Early models had wooden rear fuselages due to material shortages or to save weight, but the armoured front was never compromised and gave the aircraft (and especially the engine and crew) superb protection against small arms fire and light flak.

The Il-2 was built around the armoured cockpit section, with rear fuselage and wings being bolted directly onto it

ILYUSHIN IL-2 SHTURMOVIK

Shturmoviks over the ruins of Berlin, April 1945

The Il-2 was simple and rugged, and easily maintained in rough field conditions

A Shturmovik crew prepare for a sortie

COCKPIT

The Il-2's cockpit was basic and functional, reflecting the aircraft's own rugged and basic design. The pilot's controls were simple, and the control column had multiple firing buttons for the different weapons. The rear-gunner sat on a canvas strap rather than a proper seat, and had limited protection from the elements. The pilot's front windscreen was 55-65mm armourglass, with thinner armourglass sheets on the sides, but the rear cockpit was often left open to the elements to improve visibility. Although women flew the Shturmovik, there were no all-female units.

Right: *The Il-2's crew were protected by thick armour*

OPERATION TORCH
8-16 November 1942

Operation Torch was at the time, the largest amphibious operation in the history of warfare, in which the Western Allies opened a second front in North Africa. Three amphibious invasions were launched in Morocco and Algeria, occupied by Vichy French forces, allied with the Axis powers. Operation Torch was a gamble – although it was expected that Vichy forces in the region would not fight their former allies, many did. Nonetheless the invasion lasted only eight days, with fighting ending on 16 November. In response to the invasion, Hitler ordered the occupation of Vichy France.

KEY BATTLE

STALINGRAD
THE CITY THAT REFUSED TO DIE

The industrial heart of Soviet Russia was in fact never a German objective for Case Blue. So how did it become a turning point in the war and a devastating loss for the Nazis?

WORDS JON TRIGG & DR MICHAEL JONES

After the failure of Operation Barbarossa in the summer of 1941, the Germans had been stunned by Moscow's winter counter-offensive launched at the beginning of December. Adolf Hitler's 'stand and fight' order had saved the German Army from disintegrating in the snow, but in the dawn of the new year of 1942 the question on everyone's lips was what would Nazi Germany do next?

The answer was another offensive – Case Blue. Joseph Stalin expected the Germans to attack Moscow once again, but the Soviet dictator was wrong. According to Richard J Evans – professor of modern history at Cambridge University – Hitler was desperate for Soviet oil, believing that without it the Nazi war machine would grind to a halt as "the Third Reich remained woefully short of fuel during the war." The answer was the Soviet Union's Caucasus region, hundreds of kilometres from the current frontline but awash with oil.

Opposing forces

It was over 800km from the German Army's start line in the summer of 1942 to the oil-rich city of Grozny, now in modern-day Chechnya. To reach it Berlin realised it needed a huge offensive force that it simply couldn't muster alone after the disastrous losses of the winter. Its answer was to call on its allies to massively increase their contribution in the East. The results were astounding. The Italian contingent went from three divisions to an entire army: the 8th Army, also called the Armata Italiana in Russia or ARMIR. The Hungarians also sent a full army, the Second or Második Magyar Hadsereg, and the Romanians two: the Third and Fourth Armies. All massed under the command of Gerd von Rundstedt's Heeresgruppe Süd (Army Group South); Case Blue would comprise over 1.5 million men, along with 1,500 panzers and the same number of aircraft. Facing them would be a Soviet force of roughly the same number of aircraft, but with double the number of tanks and a million more men.

Case Blue begins

After delays imposed by pre-emptive Red Army attacks at Kharkov and the Kerch peninsula, and the capture of the Crimea, Blue finally began on 28 June 1942. A hugely complex operation, in

"BY THE BEGINNING OF AUGUST PAULUS' SIXTH ARMY HAD REACHED THE OUTSKIRTS OF THE CITY AND WAS PREPARING TO TAKE IT"

essence the plan was for the main force to break through the Soviet lines and head southeast into the Caucasus to seize the crucial oil fields.

Meanwhile, the Germans' open, northern flank would be protected by a secondary force that would drive east and reach the River Volga. Stalingrad itself was barely mentioned in the orders for the offensive, with Hitler discounting it as a major objective.

At first successful, the Germans and their allies advanced across the steppe as they had the previous summer, defeating Soviet forces as they went, but without inflicting a knockout blow.

Leading the push to the Volga was the German Sixth Army led by Friedrich Paulus, an officer described by his peer Heinz Guderian as "hard-working, original and talented" but also indecisive and "inclined to spend too much time… before issuing his orders". Nevertheless, by the beginning of August, General Paulus' Sixth Army had reached the outskirts of Stalingrad and was making preparations to take it.

Sixth Army besieges Stalingrad

Beginning on 23 August with a major air raid from the Luftwaffe's Luftflotte IV, Sixth Army attacked the city from north and south. In a succession of nightmarish attritional battles over the next two months the Germans ground forward against determined Soviet resistance.

In the south of the city the battlefield was dominated by an enormous concrete grain silo complex that towered over the surrounding area, and in the north a number of large factory complexes including the Red October and Barrikady works were fought over for weeks, with horrendous losses on both sides.

Under the inspired leadership of their commander, Vasily Chuikov, the Soviets refused to give an inch, expertly using the city's ruins to their advantage and forcing the Germans to fight the sort of close-quarter struggle that their soldiers grew to hate. As one young officer called Lieutenant Reiner despairingly wrote: "We have fought for 15 days for a single house."

The Germans used ever greater firepower to try and conquer the city; Stuka dive-bombers blasted Soviet positions while panzers and artillery fired endless shells into what was increasingly a moonscape of devastation. The respected author Jason Turner wrote in his 2012 book Stalingrad Day by Day that "the Germans expended an extraordinary amount of ammunition" which included an astonishing "911,000 artillery shells and 990,000 mortar rounds" during the fighting. Nevertheless the Soviets hung on, ferrying reinforcements over from the Volga's eastern bank and devising new tactics in their so-called 'street-fighting academies'. This included the widespread use of sniper teams, with sharpshooters like former Siberian shepherd Vasily Zaytsev becoming household names across the USSR.

Soviet sappers search for landmines, Autumn 1942

Nazi troops take cover during their assault on the city. Both sides suffered heavy losses

For their part the Germans turned to specialist combat engineer battalions: the so-called pionieren, armed with MP40 sub-machine guns, grenades and explosive charges fought to prise the Soviets out of their last positions in the Barrikady and Dzerzhinsky tractor works and in the steep ravines on the banks for the Volga.

Operation Uranus

On the night of Wednesday 18 November, fresh snow began to fall on the already-freezing soldiers of the Romanian 3rd Army far to the northwest of Stalingrad on the River Don. The German liaison officer with the Romanian IV Corps at the time was a certain Lieutenant Gerhard Stöck. A physically imposing figure, Stöck had won gold at the 1936 Berlin Olympics in the Men's Javelin and bronze in the Shot, and now he was reporting to Sixth Army headquarters that he had intelligence of an imminent Red Army offensive in this area. The report was discounted, but just before dawn on 19 November some 3,500 Soviet artillery guns received the codeword Syrene and opened fire on the Romanians. The bombardment was horrific, as the German anti-tank gunner Henry Metelmann described in his memoir Through Hell for Hitler: "All hell broke loose!... the whole bunker trembled, clods of earth fell on us and the noise was deafening." This was the opening salvoes of Georgy Zhukov's Operation Uranus.

At first the ill-equipped Romanians fought back hard, their rifle fire flaying the attacking Soviet

German troops pick their way through the city ruins. By December around 250,000 were encircled

infantry, but when the Soviets threw in their T-34/76 tanks, the lack of Romanian anti-tank guns told and their lines broke.

The following day it was the turn of the Romanian 4th Army to the south of Stalingrad to face an overwhelming Red Army assault. The German response was slow, both Paulus at Sixth Army and Armed Forces high command refusing to admit the Red Army was capable of carrying out the kind of deep-penetration operation that they themselves were masters of. Behind the front, the joint German-Romanian XXXXVIII Panzer Corps was in reserve, but in an almost unbelievable turn of events large numbers of its available panzers were immobile due to mice having gnawed through their electric cabling – their counterattack failed. Three days later the two jaws of the Soviet offensive met at Kalach on the River Don. The Germans in Stalingrad were now encircled.

The airlift

Inside the new Stalingrad Pocket were all of Sixth Army, elements of Fourth Panzer Army and several thousand Romanians from their 3rd Army. All in all some 250,000 German and allied troops were now trapped, and the question was should they attempt to break out or stand fast? Many of Paulus' senior commanders were adamant the Germans had to break out immediately when

> "SOME 250,000 GERMAN AND ALLIED TROOPS WERE NOW TRAPPED, AND THE QUESTION WAS SHOULD THEY ATTEMPT TO BREAK OUT OR STAND FAST?"

the Soviet encirclement was at its weakest, but Paulus wavered and in the end deferred to Hitler. Hermann Goering – without being in possession of the facts – told the dictator his Luftwaffe was able to supply the Pocket from the air and the decision was made that Paulus would sit tight and wait.

A figure of 300 tons of supplies per day was set as the minimum needed by Sixth Army, but with the weather worsening and a lack of available transport aircraft for the airlift, that amount was only ever achieved on a handful of occasions. In the end, the average reached only approximately a third of the requirement.

Fuel and ammunition were the priority, but as Sixth Army's own stocks dried up the besieged Germans were increasingly immobile and forced to only fire back when directly attacked. As for food, at first Sixth Army relied on its reserves and the meat from the tens of thousands of horses the troops used to pull everything from artillery pieces to ammunition wagons and store carts.

Winter Storm – the relief attempt The day after Uranus was launched, Hitler ordered the establishment of Army Group Don (Heeresgruppe Don) and put it under command of Erich von Manstein. Hitler instructed Manstein to take the offensive and relieve Sixth Army by breaking through to Stalingrad.

On 12 December Manstein launched Operation Winter Storm (Unternehmen Wintergewitter), but the weakness of his own forces, coupled with the strength of Red Army resistance, reduced the initial advance to just 19km. At the same time the Soviets keep up the pressure on the rest of the southern front, pushing the Germans back in the north and on 16 December hitting the Italian 8th Army with Operation Little Saturn. In a matter of days the Italians collapsed, with thousands fleeing to the rear across the snow-covered steppe as the Germans struggled to plug the gap.

Manstein's offensive ground on, eventually getting to within 48km of the Pocket, but wasn't strong enough to go any further. The only option was for Paulus to break out and reach Army Group Don before it was too late. In preparation

STALINGRAD

Soviet troops were under strict orders not to retreat as they faced down the German assault

for just such a move Manstein had placed 800 cargo-laden trucks at the heart of his advance. On board was 3,000 tons of fuel and ammunition to get Paulus moving and fighting and bring the bulk of his army to safety, but it wasn't to be. In scenes reminiscent of the previous month when indecision had gripped him, Paulus once again refused to act and deferred to Hitler, loudly proclaiming his battered army was incapable of reaching Manstein unless he received significant resupply beforehand.

Defeat and surrender

With Manstein unable to advance any further and Paulus refusing to break out, the fate of Sixth Army was sealed. By Christmas Eve, Red Army pressure on Army Group Don forced it to retreat – Winter Storm was over. That same day the main airfield hub for the airlift operation, Tatsinskaya (nicknamed Tazi by the Germans), fell to the Red Army's 24th Tank Corps. With no option but to now fly even further to reach the beleaguered Sixth Army, the Luftwaffe transport fleet struggled to keep on supplying the city. The day after Tazi fell only seven tons of supplies were flown in.

Four days earlier Sixth Army had reported its first case of death from starvation – a soldier in Bernhard Steinmetz's 305 Infanterie Division. One German soldier inside the Pocket wrote that "we are suffering terribly from hunger, and they are only issuing one loaf of stale bread for five men".

Conditions inside the Pocket continued to deteriorate throughout the first week of January. Ammunition was in such short supply that the 5,000 or so remaining artillery guns were only allowed to fire with permission from their responsible regimental commander, while the few remaining panzers were more or less immobile from lack of fuel. Then, on 10 January, the Red Army launched Operation Ring to finally destroy the Pocket. Three days later the Soviets attacked the Hungarian Second Army and it quickly collapsed, causing further chaos on the German southern front. On 16 January Pitomnik airfield – the main base for the airlift within the Pocket – fell to the advancing Red Army.

The Soviets offered terms to the Sixth Army, but Hitler forbade capitulation, telling Paulus: "Sixth Army will hold their positions to the last man and the last round." In an effort to stiffen his resolve, Hitler promoted Paulus to generalfeldmarschall on 30 January, knowing that no German officer of that rank had ever surrendered. Paulus saw it for what it was – an invitation to commit suicide, but he refused. Instead, the following day he walked out of his headquarters in the basement of the Univermag department store and surrendered to the Soviets.

An exhausted German soldier sits amid the ruins. One officer claimed: "We have fought for 15 days for a single house"

Nazi tanks kick up clouds of dust as they advance towards Stalingrad

KEY STRATEGY

THE ARCTIC CONVOYS

How Churchill helped save the Red Army, at great cost, but the Kremlin responded with hostile ingratitude

WORDS **ANTHONY TUCKER-JONES**

Winston Churchill was determined to help Joseph Stalin following Hitler's invasion of the Soviet Union, no matter the cost and despite their deep ideological differences. This meant that the warships of Admiral John Tovey's Home Fleet were required to escort supply convoys through the Norwegian and Barents Seas to Murmansk and Archangel. Both within the Arctic Circle, Archangel iced up from winter to spring.

Churchill and Franklin D Roosevelt, whose country had not yet entered the war, feared if they did not immediately back the battered Red Army then Stalin might rapidly sue for peace. Churchill and Roosevelt, just three months after Hitler's assault on the Soviet Union, began shipping military supplies via the Arctic. The battle of the Arctic convoys proved a bloody affair, as the Germans did everything possible to stop the intrepid sailors. These convoys were codenamed PQ – the most infamous being PQ17.

Ship after ship

"I went to Russia on the third convoy to sail from Scotland," recalled correspondent Walter Kerr of the *New York Herald Tribune*. "We left on the night of 13 October [1941], at a time when the German Army was only 65 miles [105km] from Moscow and moving so fast we did not know whether our ships would get to Russia on time." He and the convoy survived unscathed and he travelled on to the Soviet capital. The passage became more hazardous as time passed. Kerr observed: "Our ships that sailed to Russia were inadequately armed… they did not have the fire power they needed to ward off attack, but they also knew how much the supplies were needed by the Red Army. We began to lose ship after ship." It was only the arrival of a US Navy task force at Scapa Flow, after America entered the war, that helped tip the balance. At the end of May 1942 Churchill pushed through the largest Arctic convoy to date: codenamed PQ16.

Journalist Alexander Werth persuaded the editor of *The Sunday Times* to let him cover

An American ship carrying supplies to Russia is hit by the Luftwaffe north of the Arctic Circle, September 1942

THE ARCTIC CONVOYS

The crew of HMS Scylla use steam hoses to clear away ice while on patrol in the North Atlantic, 1943

the war from Moscow. Like Kerr, he experienced first-hand the desperate attempts to get military supplies to the Soviet Union. On 20 May 1942 he found himself sailing with the 10,000-ton cargo vessel Empire Baffin, which formed part of the 50-strong PQ16 convoy. The Luftwaffe was waiting for them and a week later over 100 bombers attacked southeast of Barents Island. The escort destroyers desperately did everything they could to ward off the raids. However, the bombing caused the loss of four ships and heavily damaged two others. The Luftwaffe struck twice more and just 25 vessels reached Kola Bay on the evening of 30 May. That night they were attacked again, losing another seven ships. Werth survived his baptism of fire to make his way to Moscow.

Tragedy occurred again in July 1942 with the even bigger convoy PQ17. Under threat of attack it was ordered to scatter and as a result was picked off piecemeal by U-boats and bombers. The Germans sank 24 ships along with 153 crew and 99,316 tons of supplies, plus 3,350 vehicles, 430 tanks and 210 aircraft. Brooke and Air Chief Marshal Charles Portal were vexed that valuable equipment denied to them was now at the bottom of the sea. "We kept on supplying tanks and aeroplanes that could ill be spared," grumbled Brooke, "and in doing so suffered the heaviest losses in shipping… We received nothing in return except abuse." Unlike Churchill, neither fully appreciated just how essential it was to keep the Soviet Union in the war.

Churchill found himself under pressure to postpone any further convoys until winter darkness could provide cover. He was against this, knowing full well that Stalin would be furious at any delays. Instead, he suggested to Tovey that he use his heavier warships supported by aircraft carriers to force their way through. The Royal Navy, simply could not spare the resources at a time when it was fighting the Battle of the Atlantic and pushing relief convoys through to a beleaguered Malta.

Likewise, the US Navy had its hands full in the Pacific. Reluctantly, Churchill acquiesced and signalled Stalin: "It is therefore with the greatest regret that we have reached the conclusion that to attempt to run the next convoy, PQ18, would bring no benefit to you." He then promptly changed his mind when he got Stalin's terse response, which was the usual mix of bullying and moral blackmail. PQ18 took a beating, losing 13 ships.

Churchill's deep regret

Early in 1943, under cover of the Arctic darkness, Churchill pushed through two supply convoys, but with the return of the daylight he postponed the March convoy. Then under advice from the Royal Navy he agreed that supplies by this route should stop until the return of darkness in the autumn. "This decision was taken with deep regret," he wrote later, "because of the tremendous battles on the Russian front which distinguished the campaign of 1943."

Stalin brooding in the Kremlin was far from happy with his gifts from the British Bulldog and Uncle Sam. They were simply not what he wanted. Sat at his desk he found himself reading a joint communique from Churchill and Roosevelt that caused him great displeasure. Britain and America in 1943 essentially had three options for victory: bring Germany to its knees by bombing its weapons factories, launch a European second front with an invasion of Sicily and Italy, or a cross-Channel invasion of Nazi-occupied France. The reality was that they could only manage the second with the resources available.

Stalin desperately wanted the third option, as only that would draw large numbers of German troops away from the Eastern Front. Looking at his maps, the English Channel seemed such an insignificant barrier. At the end of 1942 he had written to Roosevelt: "Permit me also to express confidence that time has not passed in vain and that the promises about opening the second front in Europe, which were given to me by you, Mr President, and Mr Churchill in relation to 1942, will be fulfilled and will anyway be fulfilled in relation to spring 1943."

After Churchill and Roosevelt's Casablanca conference in early 1943 Stalin continued to lobby them for a firm commitment to a second front. In a joint reply sent on 12 February the

Propaganda poster showing the Red Air Force protecting a British convoy arriving at Murmansk

"NOT ONLY WAS STALIN UNGRATEFUL FOR THE SUPPLIES, BUT HE ALSO DIDN'T CARE ABOUT THE WELFARE OF THE MERCHANT SAILORS WHO RISKED THEIR LIVES TO DELIVER THEM"

pair stated they were "pushing preparations to the limit of our resources for a cross-Channel operation in August… Here again shipping and assault landing craft will be limiting factors. If the operation is delayed by the weather or other reasons it will be prepared with stronger forces in September."

Stalin felt that this was too vague and pressed them to commit to the spring or early summer of 1943 at the latest. Churchill wrote back pointing out the strategic demands on their resources in the Mediterranean, the Far East, the Pacific and the Arctic convoys. Reference to the latter irked Stalin even more. He scoffed: how much time did they need? The slowing down of American and British operations in Tunisia had permitted Hitler to transfer 27 divisions from the West to the Eastern Front. Stalin was thoroughly fed up waiting for them to take the pressure off the Red Army.

Stalin livid

The Soviet leader was a wily old fox. He appreciated the one thing that Churchill and Roosevelt feared most was not so much the Soviet Union being defeated but making a separate peace deal with Hitler. If that happened they would never liberate western Europe in the face of the redeployed might of the battle-hardened Wehrmacht. In light of Stalin's victory at Stalingrad this was an unlikely outcome, nonetheless he sought to play on their fears by warning of the danger to their common cause if the second front continued to be delayed. On 15 March 1943 he cunningly signalled: "I recognise these difficulties. Nevertheless, I deem it my duty to warn you in the strongest possible manner, in the interest of our common cause, how dangerous [it] would be from the view-point of our common cause of further delay in opening a Second Front in France."

Meanwhile, Churchill and Roosevelt thrashed out how best to attack Italy. This would leave no shipping available for transporting troops and equipment to Britain in March and April, while May was also uncertain. This, plus the needs to keep supplies flowing to North Africa and preparations for an invasion of Sicily as a stepping stone to the Italian mainland, firmly ruled out any cross-Channel attack at all in 1943. Stalin knew this meant the Red Army would be on its own for another year. To further sour relations with Churchill and Roosevelt they had now closed off the Arctic supply route.

Stalin was livid that Churchill was being so difficult. In particular his decision would delay the delivery of 660 fighter aircraft. Stalin wrote to him on 2 April saying: "I consider the step as catastrophic. The Pacific and Southern [ie Iran] routes can't make up for it." Four days later Churchill replied highlighting the achievements of Bomber Command's raids against Germany's cities. He also sought to convince Stalin that the fighters would be sent via the Mediterranean as swiftly as possible.

There was another reason for the halt in the convoys. A diplomatic row broke out over the inadequacy of the air defences at Murmansk, which became the only point of access once Archangel froze. Having run the German gauntlet, the merchantmen found themselves still under attack even after they had reached their destination. Although 60 per cent of the ships were American the British had responsibility for their protection. Lobbying by Churchill failed to have the desired effect. Stalin declined to boost fighter cover over Murmansk and refused to let the RAF help. He wanted Churchill and Roosevelt to concentrate on opening a vital second front in Europe.

Stalin was perhaps understandably affronted that they insist he be grateful for the crumbs from their table. At a meeting with Generals Zhukov and Vasilevsky he had raged: "Tens, hundreds of thousands of Soviet people are giving their lives in the struggle against fascism, and Churchill is haggling over 20 Hurricanes. And their Hurricanes are no good, our pilots don't like that plane."

Kerr, who had covered the fierce battles of Moscow and Stalingrad, appreciated there was a good reason for Soviet stubbornness. He noted: "It was not an incident that astonished American and British observers in Moscow, for during all the months of aid to Russia the

In the foreground is HMS Eskimo, a Royal Navy Tribal Class Destroyer on Arctic convoy duty

A dozen Matilda tanks ready to be shipped to Russia – many ended up on the seabed

Tanks for Russia' week in which all British production went to Stalin

Russians consistently refused to allow us to operate on Russian soil. Their stand appeared inexplicable at first, but most of us came to the conclusion that it was simply a manifestation of the years of distrust that followed the revolution. The Russians would win their own war in their own way."

Desperate convoy war

Stalin cared little that the Americans and British were fighting a desperate convoy war in the Atlantic in order to supply their forces in North Africa and as part of the build-up for the second front. Hitler's submarines were now wreaking havoc on the Allies' shipping lanes. During March Admiral Karl Doenitz had over a 100 U-boats at sea and the Allies lost 700,000 tons of shipping that month. However, despite Hitler's best efforts a lot of equipment was still reaching the Soviet Union.

The Luftwaffe issued a secret intelligence report on 4 April 1943 that assessed around 1.2 million tons of supplies had got through via the Arctic route compared to just half-a-million via the Persian Gulf and the Far East. It reported: "Besides raw materials, victuals and mineral oil, it included 1,880 aircraft, 2,350 tanks, 8,300 lorries, 6,400 other vehicles and 2,250 guns." According to Werth this assessment was remarkably accurate. He noted that American deliveries during 1941-42 amounted to 1.2 million tons and British shipments 532,000 tons.

Kerr in 1943 reckoned that in the first year of deliveries Churchill and Roosevelt supplied Stalin with 4,084 tanks, 3,052 planes, 30,031 vehicles and 831,000 tons of miscellaneous goods. Regardless of all the sacrifice to get it there the Red Army found much of what it received was obsolete. Over half the tanks delivered in 1942 were thinly armoured and insufficiently armed light tanks. The following year the proportion rose to 70 percent. Even the heavy tanks such as the British Matilda were found wanting and "as inflammable as a box of matches".

It was evident to Werth from his contacts in Moscow that it was Uncle Sam's gifts that were going to have the biggest impact on the impeding fighting at Kursk in the summer of 1943. He wrote: "On 11 June I recorded a conversation with a Russian correspondent who had just been to Kursk. He said the Russian equipment there was truly stupendous; he had never seen anything like it. What was also going to make a big difference this summer was the enormous number of American trucks."

Incredible generosity

Armoured vehicles supplied by America, Britain and Canada represented a sizable chunk of the Red Army's tank forces. By the end of the war some 22,800 armoured vehicles had been provided, of which 1,981 were lost at sea with the Arctic convoys.

These deliveries represented about 16 percent of Soviet tank production, 12 percent of self-propelled guns and all armoured personnel carrier production. The first shipment in 1941 totalled 487 British Matilda, Valentine and Tetrarch tanks and 182 American M3A1 light tanks and M3 Lee medium tanks. The following year these shipments had increased to 2,497 from Britain and 3,023 from America. Yet Stalin still remained unmoved by such generosity.

Although the Red Army viewed the Lend-Lease vehicles as a blessing and a curse in equal measure, there was no getting away from them. By 1943 around 20 percent of Stalin's tank brigades had Lend-Lease vehicles, while 10 percent were completely equipped with them. What was of greatest value to the Red Army were undoubtedly the trucks and lorries which significantly enhanced its mobility. Werth noted: "From my personal observation I can say that, from 1943 on, the Red Army unquestionably appreciated the help from the West – whether in the form of Airacobras, Kittyhawks, Dodges, jeeps, Spam, army boots, or medicines. The motor vehicles were particularly admired and valued."

President Franklin D Roosevelt and Prime Minister Winston Churchill at Casablanca with senior military officers

★ 14 JANUARY 1943 ★

THE CASABLANCA CONFERENCE

Western Allied leaders met in early 1943 to chart the course of WWII in Europe and the Pacific

WORDS MICHAEL E HASKEW

THE CASABLANCA CONFERENCE

THE TIDE TURNS
1943

In the fourth year of the war, fascist Italy faced the first major Allied invasions, while the German high watermark was reached in the climactic Battle of Kursk. At sea, the War in the Atlantic saw a critical shift as Grand Admiral Karl Dönitz's U-boat fleet suffered catastrophic losses, and the Anglo-American alliance strengthened their strategy for victory.

Casablanca, on Morocco's Atlantic coast, was the venue of the major Allied conference between 14-24 January 1943. Early on, US President Franklin D Roosevelt and Prime Minister Winston Churchill agreed to prioritise the defeat of Nazi Germany. Imperial Japan, they reasoned, could be finally dealt with once Hitler and his henchmen were no longer a threat. This emphasis on the defeat of the Nazis was influenced by the Western pledge to continue offensive operations that would inevitably draw German manpower and other resources away from the Eastern Front, where the Soviets were bearing the brunt of the battle against the Nazis and sustaining immense casualties.

With Joseph Stalin demanding a second front in Western Europe, Roosevelt and Churchill cast their strategic eye across the Mediterranean. While the president and his senior advisors advocated the establishment of a second front in France at the earliest possible date, Churchill was reluctant to commit to such a venture in 1943, arguing the following year would be more opportune for a cross-Channel invasion. Churchill asserted, to the consternation of many within the American delegation, that until sufficient men, materiel and logistics could be established in Britain the success of any operation in Western Europe would be in doubt.

In the end, the British point of view prevailed. Churchill proposed a continuation of the Mediterranean strategy, a strike at the supposedly 'soft underbelly' of Nazi and fascist Europe. It was agreed that the next Allied offensive thrust would take place against Sicily, codenamed Operation Husky. In concert with the preparations for Husky, a massive disinformation campaign would also be mounted in order to divert German forces to Greece, Sardinia, the Balkans or even France.

The Allies further agreed that once Sicily had been secured, an amphibious landing would take place on the Italian mainland, opening the second front in 1943 – just not where Stalin had expected. Nevertheless, the build-up for the invasion of Western Europe would continue and the intensity of the strategic bombing of Nazi-occupied territory would be stepped up, hopefully laying waste to the enemy's industrial capacity and demoralising the German people as their cities were devastated. The transfer of war materiel and supplies to the Soviet Union would remain a priority.

In the Pacific, the leaders agreed to the continuation of the joint effort to eject the Japanese from Papua, New Guinea, while a vital overland supply route should be established from India to China as the fighting continued in Japanese-controlled Burma. From a global perspective and for media and morale consumption, the focal point of the Casablanca Conference was a joint declaration that only the unconditional surrender of the Axis powers would be an acceptable outcome of the war. There would be no negotiated peace or terms offered such as had occurred with the armistice of the First World War.

The Allied leaders also stressed at Casablanca that unconditional surrender did not extend to the brutalisation and extermination of the German, Italian and Japanese peoples. To that end, they qualified their declaration with the statement that their war aims were focused on "the destruction of the philosophies in those countries which are based on conquest and the subjugation of other peoples".

KEY BATTLE

INVASION OF SICILY
THE 'SOFT UNDERBELLY'

In Summer 1943, Allied forces invaded the Axis homeland for the first time in a huge, complex operation that involved airborne and amphibious landings

WORDS **TOM GARNER**

By 1943, the Allies were beyond what Winston Churchill referred to as the "perhaps, the end of the beginning" of the Second World War. Axis forces had finally been driven out of North Africa and Allied commanders turned their attention to the wider strategy in the Mediterranean. With the Soviet Union fighting a brutal war against the Nazis on the Eastern Front, the Western Allies were expected to open a second front in Europe. The question was: where?

It was Churchill who advocated an invasion of Italy. Famously referring to the then-fascist country as the "soft underbelly of Europe", the British prime minister believed that knocking Italy out of the war had several benefits. Neutral Turkey could potentially join the Allies and Italy would be a useful springboard for Allied invasions into Austria and Germany. At worst, the campaign in Italy would divert precious Axis resources away from the vast Eastern Front.

Although Churchill was enthusiastic about Italy, the United States was not. The Americans wanted to pour their European war resources into an invasion of northern France, which eventually became Operation Overlord. However, they did agree to invade Italy alongside their British partners with the first target being the country's most southerly region: Sicily.

Codenamed Operation Husky, the island invasion of Sicily was critical to a future assault on the Italian mainland. Using hundreds of thousands of troops, Husky was actually the largest Allied amphibious invasion of the war. It was also innovative, with the Allies launching large airborne operations for the first time and successfully deploying pioneering landing craft. However, despite their numerical and technological advantage, the Allies met larger than expected resistance and argued among themselves. The "soft underbelly" turned out to be not so soft after all.

Allied troops wade ashore in Sicily during Operation Husky, the success of which was crucial to a future assault on the Italian mainland

INVASION OF SICILY

British airborne soldiers pictured in an Airspeed Horsa glider just before they fly to Sicily

OPERATION LADBROKE

The British conducted the first mass Allied airborne landing of the Second World War in a hazardous but successful operation to capture Syracuse. Prior to the invasion of Sicily, airborne operations during the war had been pioneered by German forces. The Fallschirmjäger branch of the Luftwaffe conducted combat airborne attacks during their invasions of Norway, the Netherlands and – most infamously – Crete. The Allies took careful note of these successes, with Churchill stating that airborne warfare was now a means "to be able to storm a series of water obstacles… everywhere from the Channel to the Mediterranean and in the East".

The British quickly developed their own airborne forces, including the Parachute Regiment and Glider Pilot Regiment. These, among other units, were formed into the 1st Airborne Division in 1941. Among the division's five brigades was the 1st Airlanding Brigade and 1st Parachute Brigade. These two brigades would participate in the invasion of Sicily and make Allied airborne history.

During complex planning in the build-up to the invasion, the Allies decided that the British would use three airborne brigades to capture the Ponte Grande and Primasole bridges as well as the port of Augusta. Meanwhile, units from the US 82nd Airborne Division would be dropped northeast of the port of Gela to prevent Axis reserves from attacking the Allied beaches.

The British decided to first capture the Ponte Grande bridge south of Syracuse. This mission, known as Operation Ladbroke, was to be conducted immediately prior to the amphibious landings on the night of 9 July 1943 under the command of Brigadier Philip Hicks, the commander of 1st Airlanding Brigade. As well as capturing Ponte Grande, the brigade was also tasked with securing Syracuse – particularly the city's harbour.

"USING HUNDREDS OF THOUSANDS OF TROOPS, HUSKY WAS ACTUALLY THE LARGEST ALLIED AMPHIBIOUS INVASION OF WWII"

Ladbroke was initially designed to involve paratroopers but Field Marshal Bernard Montgomery altered the plan so it would be a glider operation instead. This would primarily use infantry, with smaller numbers of artillery and engineers. Using gliders was risky, especially because the Allies were relatively inexperienced in airborne operations. Some RAF officers argued that a night glider operation would be impractical, while pilots from the Glider Pilot Regiment had to build their own aircraft.

Nevertheless, 144 American WACO CG-4 gliders, along with a small number of British Airspeed Horsa gliders, would transport over 2,000 British soldiers to Sicily from North Africa. Lieutenant Bernard H Halsall of the Glider Pilot Regiment recalled: "We had just over a week to study photographs and for all the other activities in preparation for the attack, culminating in a church service… This would be the first return to European soil by the Allies since Dunkirk."

On the evening of 9 July 1943, the first British gliders took off from North Africa and were towed to Sicily by United States Army Air

Right, top: American paratroopers of US 82nd Airborne Division depart for daylight parachute drops over Sicily, 10 July 1943

Right, middle: American paratroopers jump from their Dakota aircraft over Sicily, 10 July 1943

Right, bottom: RAF instructors teach NCOs of the Glider Pilot Regiment to pilot troop-carrying gliders at a training school near Oxford, 8 October 1942

Forces (USAAF) Dakota aircraft. The visibility was poor, with glider pilots often losing sight of the Dakotas' safety lights. When the time came for the gliders to land, only 12 reached their designated landing zones. The majority landed some distance away, and many soldiers drowned when their gliders landed in the sea after being prematurely released from the Dakotas.

Halsall's WACO glider crashed. "We crossed the shoreline and flew on into the darkness," he recalled. "We hit the first tree of the olive grove at about 80mph [130kp/h]. Several minutes later, after we had all regained consciousness… we moved off in the direction of the firing."

One glider crew managed to capture Ponte Grande without difficulty but because most of the other aircraft had crashed or missed their landing zones, only a few dozen British soldiers (including Halsall) were able to defend the bridge from Italian forces. The British faced hundreds of Italian soldiers from 385th Coastal Battalion and 75th (Napoli) Infantry Regiment. Halsall recalled: "During the rest of the night and throughout the morning the enemy launched a series of vicious counterattacks." Such was the ferocity of the fighting that there were less than a dozen British soldiers left, including Halsall, on the afternoon of the second day of fighting. These men surrendered to the Italians but they were liberated in less than an hour by forward troops of the British Eighth Army who had landed during the amphibious operation.

The Eighth Army took Ponte Grande and Halsall was awarded the Military Cross for his bravery. His citation read: "He took over the defence of the Syracuse bridge and throughout several counterattacks showed coolness and courage and was an inspiration to all. It was due to his leadership that his sector held for 15 hours and credit showed to Lieutenant Halsall that the operation as a whole was a success."

Operation Ladbroke had indeed been a success but it came at a price. Around 25% of the airborne troops had become casualties, including 313 killed and 174 missing or wounded. In the aftermath of Ladbroke, the British increased training for glider pilots and no longer allowed gliders to be released at night over water. Inter-aircraft communication was also improved, and aircrews were trained in both glider and paratrooper operations.

Nevertheless, despite Ladbroke's costly shortcomings, Halsall recognised its importance: "History had been made that night of the 9th July 1943. This was the first mass landing by glider behind enemy lines by the Allies. Four more were to follow before the end of hostilities."

> "WE HIT THE FIRST TREE OF THE OLIVE GROVE AT ABOUT 80MPH. SEVERAL MINUTES LATER, AFTER WE HAD ALL REGAINED CONSCIOUSNESS… WE MOVED OFF IN THE DIRECTION OF THE FIRING"

STORMY LANDINGS

Contrary to popular belief, D-Day was not the largest amphibious Allied invasion of the Second World War. It was actually the Sicilian coast that saw the most Allied soldiers go ashore, on 9 July 1943. During the Normandy landings, 156,000 Allied troops landed on enemy territory but for Sicily over 180,000 soldiers were deployed. The geographical breadth of the Allied invasion was also huge, with the Allies landing on 26 beaches along 105 miles (170km) of coastline.

Operation Husky was a truly international undertaking. Led by the Americans and British, the multinational Allied force also included Canadian, Free French, Indian and Australian troops along with some Sicilian partisans. Thousands of ships were also required to ferry the soldiers but the Allies first needed to have control of the air over Sicily. After the recapture of Tunisia, Allied bombers conducted tens of thousands of sorties against Axis airfields in southern Italy, Sardinia and particularly Sicily. By 9 July 1943, only two Axis airfields on the island remained operational.

Allied troops, guns and transport are rushed ashore ready for action, 10 July 1943

With air superiority seemingly confirmed, the Allies focussed their plans on the amphibious landings, which involved 3,200 Allied vessels – the majority being from either the Royal Navy or US Navy. On the landing crafts, there would not just be hundreds of thousands of soldiers but also hundreds of tanks and thousands more mechanised vehicles.

Opposing the Allies on Sicily were numerically superior Axis soldiers; 230,000 of these were Italian troops organised into coastal defence units while the Germans consisted of two divisions commanded by General Hans-Valentin Hube. The Italians had lost many of their best soldiers in North Africa but General Dwight D Eisenhower refused to be complacent. This would be the first time that an Axis nation would be defending its home soil, and the Allied high command knew very well that this could more than likely cause the Italians to fight with even greater ferocity.

The airborne operations were conducted on the night of 9-10 July 1943, with the seaborne landings beginning on the morning of 10 July. All Allied forces would land on the southern

INVASION OF SICILY

Soldiers stand up to their waists in water unloading stores while beach roads are prepared for heavy and light traffic, 10 July 1943

Eighth Army troops wade ashore onto the Sicilian coast from a landing craft

coast of Sicily, with the US Seventh Army landing on beaches around Licata, Gela and Scoglitti. Meanwhile, the British Eighth Army would land further east on beaches in the vicinity of Pachino and Syracuse.

The day of the invasion was hampered by adverse weather conditions. A storm caused heavy winds as the first Allied troops landed from 2.45am on 10 July. This made the amphibious landings difficult but the inclement weather surprised the Italian and German defenders, who believed that landings would not be attempted in such conditions. Allied vessels also had to contend with hidden shoals off the coast that delayed some landings by several hours.

Protected by six battleships, ten cruisers and two aircraft carriers, the Allies were able to successfully land on their beaches, despite the geographical distance between many of them. They were also greatly helped by their six-wheeled DUKW amphibious vehicles. Nicknamed 'Ducks', the DUKWs had only been in production since 1942 and Sicily was their first major operation. Hundreds were available for the invasion and they performed well. The American military magazine *Stars and Stripes* even reported that when Italian soldiers saw the vehicles emerging from the water they surrendered out of amazement.

BATTLE OF GELA

Yet this anecdote does not accurately represent how Axis forces responded to the invasion of the island. In many places the Italians and Germans fought fiercely, particularly at Gela. Located in the American landing sector, what became known as the Battle of Gela was fought during 10-12 July.

The Americans came under heavy attack by Axis forces at Gela, with German and Italian aircraft and tanks attacking ships and landing soldiers. The Americans suffered 2,300 casualties and the loss of the destroyer USS Maddox, which was bombed and sunk. These attacks continued until American soldiers captured Ponte Olivo Airfield. The Germans incurred hundreds of losses at Gela but the Italians suffered even more – over 10,000 casualties, including around 3,350 killed.

Elsewhere, Axis aircraft were still able to wreak havoc against the invaders despite diminished numbers. German aircraft sank the minesweeper USS Sentinel off Licata as well as the American landing ship LST-313.

Italian Stukas also sank the British hospital ship HMHS Talamba, although all 400 of its wounded patients were safely evacuated.

Despite these setbacks, the seaborne landings were successful. During 10-14 July, hundreds of thousands of troops were disembarked from thousands of ships and covered by over 4,000 aircraft. General Sir Harold Alexander, the overall commander of Allied ground forces, was then able to establish a line from Licata in the west to Catania in the east from which the Allies could then operate to capture the rest of the island.

American cargo ship SS Robert Rowan explodes after being hit by a German bomb off Gela, 11 July 1943

★ **KEY TECH** ★

SUPERMARINE SPITFIRE

This iconic fighter plane is most famous as the saviour of Britain in 1940, but that was just the start of its remarkable story

WORDS **STUART HADAWAY**

SUPERMARINE SPITFIRE

YEARS BUILT 1936-51
LENGTH 9.58M (31FT 5IN)
WINGSPAN 11.23M (36FT 10IN)
MAXIMUM SPEED 644KM/H (400MPH)
RANGE 724KM (450 MILES)
ENGINE ROLLS-ROYCE / PACKARD MERLIN 266
CREW 1
ARMAMENT 4-8 x .303 BROWNING MACHINE GUNS, 2 x 20MM HISPANO CANNON, 500LB (227KG) BOMB

The enduring Spitfire design means it the only Allied fighter built during the war that was used until the 1950s. Over 20,000 were built in total

SUPERMARINE SPITFIRE

This MK IIa P7350 is the only Spitfire that fought in the Battle of Britain and is still airworthy

Pilots of the 611 West Lancashire Squadron launching a Spitfire off Biggin Hill Airport in 1942

"PART OF MITCHELL'S GENIUS WAS TO BRING ALL OF THESE ELEMENTS TOGETHER, AND MUCH OF THE SPITFIRE'S GREATNESS LAY IN THE UNDERLYING STRENGTH OF THE BASIC DESIGN"

The Supermarine Spitfire Mk. 1 entered service with the Royal Air Force (RAF) in 1938. It was the RAF's most modern fighter; sleek, fast, heavily armed, and beautiful. Two years later, with the Hawker Hurricane, it formed the frontline of Britain's defence against the German Luftwaffe, and while it proved arguably the most successful of the British or German fighters involved, it was only narrowly.

The Supermarine Spitfire was designed by a team led by the brilliant Reginald Mitchell, incorporating the latest technology from across the aviation industry. The elliptical wing was designed by Canadian Beverley Shenstone, while the under-wing radiators had been pioneered by the Royal Aircraft Establishment (RAE). The monocoque structure, where the aluminium skin bore much of the load, had been developed by a range of designers before being perfected in America. The engine was provided by Rolls Royce, their new 1,030hp Merlin II.

Part of Mitchell's genius was to bring all of these elements together, and much of the Spitfire's greatness lay in the underlying strength of the basic design. Time would prove that all manner of extra elements could be altered.

The type first flew in 1936, and entered squadron service in 1938, a year after Mitchell's early death. The modifications began almost immediately. Even before the Battle of Britain 100-octane fuel was introduced, giving an increase in speed, and later selected Mk. Is were fitted with different propellers to also improve performance. Most adaptations and upgrades came from combat experience in 1940.

43

COCKPIT

The cockpit features a spade-like control column and the throttle control is located in the sidewall

"PILOTS PAST AND PRESENT HAVE COMMENTED FAVOURABLY ON ITS EASE OF HANDLING AS WELL AS THE ICONIC SOUND OF ITS ENGINE"

The aircraft that embodies the spirit and resolve of the British in the summer of 1940 is remarkably easy to pilot. Easy to start, the Merlin engine nearly always fired after two blades and was very reliable with each and every cockpit virtually identical and compact.

Pilots past and present have commented favourably on its ease of handling as well as the iconic sound of its engine. As with many aircraft of the era, the Spitfire became harder to control when it neared its top speed. However its light control column allowed it to be more maneuverable than its rival, the Messerschmitt 109. During the Battle of Britain it would often turn out of dives much quicker than its German equivalent. Without powered controls, these turns were achieved by the pilot's muscle power alone.

ARMAMENT

In early models, two wing-mounted cannons were only equipped with 60 rounds each, meaning that the pilot had to be especially careful not to waste ammo – 60 rounds was only enough for around 30 seconds of cumulative fire.

In addition, two .303 machine guns were mounted in each wing to support the heavier cannon fire, although ammunition was limited. Pilots were encouraged to fire in two- to three-second bursts to conserve rounds

The most numerous Mk V model came in three main variants depending on the armament fit. Type A wings had eight .303 machine guns; the Type B had two 20mm Hispano cannon plus four Brownings; the Type C had fittings for either configuration. This production of multiple wings became standard from 1941. All types could also carry a 500lb (227kg) bomb.

.303 machine guns and Hispano cannons were mounted under the wings

SPITFIRE VS HURRICANE
WHICH BATTLE OF BRITAIN MACHINE WAS THE SUPERIOR FIGHTER CRAFT?

SUPERMARINE SPITFIRE

ENGINE

The Spitfire is sleeker than the Hurricane, giving it more agility and a better top speed

After the Battle of Britain, the Spitfire assumed more of a reconnaissance role and was even occasionally painted pink to add to its camouflage

In a modern redesign, part of the engine was moved to make way for the second cockpit on trainer models

Despite being used in more than 40 aircraft during World War II, the Rolls Royce Merlin is most commonly associated with the Spitfire. The engine first took to the skies in February 1935 and was a marked improvement on the previous Rolls Royce instalment, the Kestrel.

The engine was so good that both the Spitfire and the Hurricane were built to accommodate it.

As efficient as it was, the Merlin wasn't fuel-injected, so was prone to cutting out in steep dives. However, this was mostly fixed in 1941 by the addition of a new diaphragm in the engine's float chamber. This was affectionately known as the 'Miss Shilling's Orifice' after its designer Tilly Shilling. Production of Merlin engines only ceased in 1950.

THE MESSERSCHMITT BF 109

Fresh from its preparation in the Condor Legion in the Spanish Civil War, the Luftwaffe's Messerschmitts were ready to take the battle to the British over the Channel. 33,000 were made in total during the war and it provided the spine of the Luftwaffe fleet. Unlike the Spitfire, the Messerschmitt only had two machine guns but these contained magazines of 1,000 rounds each.

They also had two 20mm cannon that were useful against bombers but struggled to cope with the maneuverability of Spitfires and Hurricanes. Its main Achilles heel was its short range, which prevented it from doing more damage across the Channel. Despite its loss in the Battle of Britain, the Bf 109 shot down the most Allied planes in the war and the design was taken on in 1947 by the new state of Israel. Its longevity was down to its simple and direct design and it was still frequently used even in the later years of the war when the jet powered Me 262 arrived.

Images: Alamy, Boultbee Flight Academy, Getty

SUPERMARINE SPITFIRE
- ★ **MAXIMUM SPEED** 608KM/H (378MPH)
- **RATE OF CLIMB** 812M (2,665FT) PER MIN
- **CEILING** 10,668M (35,000FT)
- ★ **ARMAMENT** 2 x 20MM HISPANO MK II CANNONS
  4 x .303 CAL BROWNING MACHINE GUNS
  2 x 240LB BOMBS
- ★ **LONGEVITY** 1938-48 (20,351 MADE)

HAWKER HURRICANE
- 547KM/H (340MPH) **MAXIMUM SPEED**
- 847M (2,780FT) PER MIN **RATE OF CLIMB** ★
- 10,972M (36,000FT) **CEILING** ★
- 4 x 20MM HISPANO MK II CANNONS **ARMAMENT**
  2 x 250LB BOMBS OR
  1 x 500LB BOMB
- 1937-44 (14,583 MADE) **LONGEVITY**

The Hawker Hurricane served in all major theatres of World War II

KEY STRATEGY

DEATH OF THE WOLFPACKS

In May 1943, the Allies combined new tactics and technological innovations to devastate Germany's U-boat fleet, finally gaining the upper hand in the Atlantic campaign

WORDS **MARK WOOD**

By the end of WWII, Germany's U-boat arm had a casualty rate of 70 percent

DEATH OF THE WOLFPACKS

A U-boat is attacked by a US aircraft. Minutes after this photo was taken the vessel was sunk

By the close of 1942, Allied shipping losses in the Atlantic had reached a peak, with 1,006 ships sunk by U-boat wolfpacks that year. Many of them were destroyed in the Greenland Gap, the area of mid-Atlantic which was out of range of protective Allied air cover.

The following year brought radical changes to the Allied tactical and strategic struggle against the U-boats, with new training, technology and weapons, culminating in a catastrophic month of destruction for the German U-boat fleet. The Kriegsmarine lost more boats during the month of May 1943 than in the entire year of 1941, prompting its senior officers and later historians to remember it as Black May.

On the first day of May 1943, the Kriegsmarine's Oberkommando der Marine recorded a total of 134 submarines at sea. Of those, 118 were on station or deploying to rendezvous, with 58 boats in four battle groups already positioned in the North Atlantic. The U-boats had transited from bases on the French and Baltic coasts to gather as the largest submarine force assembled at sea. Their operational mission was to destroy the merchant fleets sailing in convoy to supply Britain from the United States and Canada. The boats' captains were driven on by the commander of the German U-boat arm Grand Admiral Karl Dönitz's exhortation: "Angreifen! Ran! Versenken!" ("Attack! Advance! Sink!")

Ranged against them were elements of the combined Allied navies supported by the formidable industrial base of the United States and RAF Coastal Command, which included British and Commonwealth aircrew manning a variety of anti-submarine aircraft. In the words of Sir John Slessor, appointed commander in chief Coastal Command in February 1943, these men were "fighting the elements as much as the enemy, but when the tense moment came, going in undaunted, going in at point-blank range against heavy fire, knowing full well that if they were shot down into the cruel sea, their chances of survival were slender".

From January 1943, Coastal Command's meagre resources were augmented by a squadron of Consolidated B24 Liberator four-engined bombers. The Liberator proved a godsend for the Allied convoys plying their way back and forth across the Atlantic. Its additional fuel tanks extended the aircraft's range to 3,000 miles (4,830km) and Iceland-based squadrons were able to close the Greenland Gap, enabling constant air cover across the Atlantic.

It was a Liberator bomber that claimed the second victim of Black May. On the 4th, U109, a veteran of four wolfpacks, captained by Oberleutnant zur See Joachim Schramm, a highly regarded former 1936 Olympic athlete, was intercepted on the surface transiting south-west of Ireland by a Liberator of 89 Squadron. Dropping a pattern of four depth charges, the crew of the Liberator initially assumed they had been unsuccessful; however, U109 was then observed slowly sinking beneath the waves, and despite her slow descent none of the crew emerged and all were assumed lost with the boat.

Both U258 and U304 also fell victim to a Liberator, the former on 20 May, depth-charged, rather appropriately, off Cape Farewell, Greenland. U304 was caught eight days later in the same area. Both were sunk by aircraft of 120 Squadron RAF. A further seven U-boats were claimed by flying boats of both the United States Navy (USN) and the RAF. The most successful of these patrol bombers were the Short Sunderland, which sank three submarines during May, and the Consolidated PBY Catalina, which destroyed four more.

On 14 May U640 was sighted by Catalina K of USN 84 Squadron, patrolling out of Reykjavik, Iceland. The crew located the U-boat some 16 miles (26km) ahead of an approaching convoy. Approaching low from the surfaced U-boat's port beam, the Catalina released three 350lb (160kg) depth bombs from a height of 75ft (23m), set with shallow fuses. The depth bombs straddled the U-boat, which was then observed to slow to two knots, trailing air bubbles, before listing at an angle and sinking with its entire crew of 56.

During the first years of the Second World War, Royal Navy use of ASDIC (active sonar detection equipment) in anti-submarine warfare (ASW) was

A US Navy PBY Catalina flying boat over the Atlantic

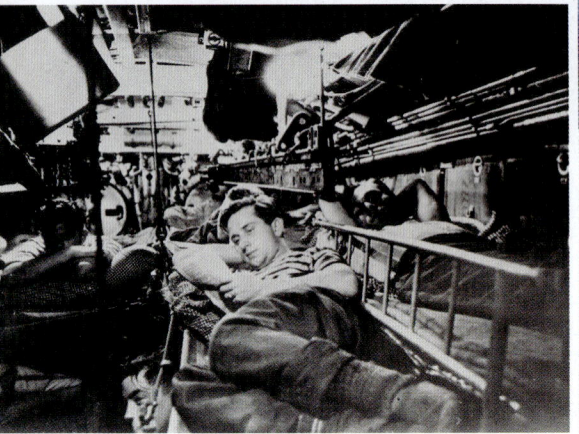

Left: The forward mess space on a U-boat, illustrating the cramped conditions endured by crewmen

dictated by the deployment of depth charges from astern. This required the ship to pass over the intended target before dropping depth charges from racks sited astern; the resultant explosions disrupted ASDIC, rendering the hunter effectively blind for some time after and making relocation of enemy contacts very difficult.

Captain Frederic John Walker, popularly known as 'Johnny', was born in Plymouth in 1896 and joined the Royal Navy in 1909, spending the First World War as an officer onboard destroyers. During the post-war period, Walker took an interest in sub-surface operations and took courses at the new anti-submarine warfare school HMS Osprey in Dorset. He understood that, rather than rely on passive defence, it was imperative to aggressively take the fight to the enemy and he was instrumental in creating the five support groups which used tactical mobility to reinforce areas of a convoy under attack and actively hunt the predators.

Walker adapted to the problem of ASDIC blindness by devising what he called the creeping attack. Having located a U-boat at depth, a directing ship trailed the submarine at a distance of 1,500 to 2,000 yards while the attacking ship, acting on instructions from the directing ship by radio, took up station between the directing ship and target at a speed of five knots and dropped depth charges, immediately clearing the target area at speed. The directing ship was able to detect any evasive action by the submarine and then dropped a further pattern of depth charges over the target. The slow approach of the attacking vessel left the U-boat commander unaware of the impending launch of depth charges and also protected the attacking ship from the latest German acoustic torpedoes, which were ineffective against ships travelling at low speeds.

The plaster attack was a variation on the creeping attack, utilising four vessels rather than two. Three ships sailed in line abreast formation over the U-boat, directed by a fourth vessel behind them; the centre ship of the three attackers positioned directly over the submarine, so that any evasive left or right turn by the U-boat commander brought them under another attacker and further depth charges.

Walker believed in an unrelenting training schedule that drove his crews to exhaustion but which firmly instilled the ASW doctrine and skills needed in the Atlantic struggle. The Royal Navy was also the first to create extensive ASW training facilities and produced the attack trainer, a simulator which reproduced conditions at sea and put officers and ASDIC operators through their paces in a realistic warfare environment.

At Western Approaches Command in Liverpool, Captain Gilbert Roberts had realised that U-boats were infiltrating into the convoy formation, firing their torpedoes then submerging to wait while the convoy passed overhead. Roberts devised a tactic with the unlikely name of Raspberry, which called for escort ships to trail the convoy and attack the U-boat once it had resurfaced after the convoy had passed and the commander assumed it was safe.

By March 1943, the Allies had reached their lowest ebb. During this month the four-day battle between U-boats and Allied escort vessels for convoy HX229/SC122, on its way from New York to Britain, resulted in the sinking of 22 merchant ships for the loss of a single U-boat. At the end of March over half-a-million tonnes of shipping had disappeared into the dark waters of the Atlantic. During April 1943, a further quarter-of-a-

Submarine at sea 1943, by German artist Adolf Bock, depicts a U-boat in choppy conditions, with crew members on the conning tower

DEATH OF THE WOLFPACKS

million tonnes were lost. The Admiralty in London acknowledged that the German submarine arm had come perilously close to entirely 'disrupting communications' across the Atlantic Ocean.

It was towards the end of April that the most significant struggle of that year began, which would continue on into the month the Kriegsmarine would later christen Black May: the battle for convoy ONS5. The convoy of 42 freighters and tankers, sailing in ballast or loaded with goods, was routed from Liverpool to Halifax, Nova Scotia, departing Britain on 21 April 1943. Two wolfpacks, Star and Fink (Finch) totalling 43 U-boats, attempted to penetrate the escort group B7's mixed screen of seven destroyers, frigates and corvettes led by Commander Peter Gretton RN, and attack the vulnerable ships lumbering their way through the Atlantic swell.

The slow speed of the convoy made necessary by the inclement weather and heavy sea state conserved fuel oil but made refuelling from the accompanying tankers impossible. Leading Sick Berth Attendant Howard Goldsmith onboard HMS Snowflake remembered: "There were times there when the convoy was literally stationary because some of the merchant ships couldn't make headway against the wind and the sea." Escort vessels averaged a fuel consumption of eight percent daily, rendering the convoy extremely vulnerable to foul weather which also forced many ships off course, thereby requiring the escorts of B7 to chase stragglers back into position.

ONS5 reached the Star wolfpack patrol sector on the morning of 28 April, being observed and reported by U650. Maintaining contact with the convoy, U650's presence was augmented by four further U-boats; however, her contact reports had warned Gretton of the threat, and HF DF radio-direction finding detected an arc of enemy vessels from the port beam round to astern of the convoy.

Three days into the voyage, a B17 Flying Fortress of 206 Squadron RAF from Benbecula air base in the Outer Hebrides located the German submarine U710 on the surface south of Iceland and some 10 miles (16km) ahead of ONS5. It engaged with a pattern of depth charges and the U-boat commander made the unwise decision to fight back with the boat's 3.5in (88mm) naval gun – the unequal fight concluded with the loss of U710 and her entire crew of 49. This encouraging early success was merely a precursor to a rapid series of U-boat kills, and Walker's anti-submarine tactics and training were about to prove extremely fruitful for the escort vessels of the Royal Navy.

On 5 May, while providing close escort to convoy ONS5, HMS Sunflower, a Flower-class corvette, picked up the Type VIIC boat U638 on ASDIC south of Greenland and proceeded to mount a creeping attack with her Hedgehog weapons system. Mortally damaged, the U-boat was able to transmit a last desperate signal stating it had been hit and was sinking. Nothing further was heard and U638 was lost with all hands. In the early hours of the following day, HMS Loosestrife, a Flower-class corvette, tracking a contact east of the coast of Labrador, dropped a spread of depth charges which sank the ill-fated Type IXC/40 U192 commanded by Oberleutnant zur See Werner Happe, killing its entire crew. U192 had sailed from Kiel on 13 April on her maiden voyage and was perhaps the most short-lived U-boat of the war, its first and only patrol lasting just 23 days.

Black May grew darker still for the head of Germany's navy when on 19 May the Type VIIC boat U954, tracked by the sloop HMS Sennen and frigate HMS Jed, was attacked with the Hedgehog mortar system and sunk in a classic creeping attack. A veteran of five wolfpacks, U954 was sent to the bottom with her entire crew, among them Leutnant zur See Peter Doenitz, the youngest son of the grand admiral.

On the 21 May U303 was ordered to depart her home port of Toulon on the French coast and join the Mediterranean U-boat fleet. Sailing from port, U303 was intercepted by the British S-class submarine HMS Sickle and hit by two torpedoes, reportedly sinking in less than 30 seconds in a rare clash of sub-surface vessels.

Two further U-boat losses on 25 and 26 May brought the total loss to 43: 25 percent of operational U-boat strength, the majority in the Atlantic and Biscay approaches. The losses that month were ruinous for all protagonists. The Royal Navy's escort ships may have emerged unscathed, but 58 merchant vessels were sunk with catastrophic loss of life. Allied shipping losses in the Atlantic dropped to 284 for 1943 for the destruction of 237 U-boats, and to 31 ships the following year with 242 U-boats sunk.

By the summer of 1943 the morale of U-boat crews was in freefall and the seasoned wolves of the Atlantic had become resigned to their fate. Meeting with Hitler at the Führer's Berghof residence in Obersalzburg on 31 May, Dönitz lamented: "These losses are too high. We must conserve our strength, otherwise we will play into the hands of the enemy." It wasn't until 15 years after Germany's defeat that Dönitz, who survived the war and at Nuremberg was sentenced to 10 years in prison, was able to acknowledge the decisive turning point in the war at sea. Referring to Black May, he admitted bluntly: "We had lost the Battle of the Atlantic."

Top left: A Type VII U-Boat is attacked from the air, c. 1943
Above: A 24-barrelled anti-submarine mortar nicknamed a Hedgehog
Below: V-Class Destroyer HMS Vidette served in convoy escort duties

KEY TECH

T-34 MEDIUM TANK

This simple but effective design changed the balance of armoured power on the Eastern Front

WORDS **MIKE HASKEW**

The T-34 medium tank made its combat debut with the Soviet Red Army in the autumn of 1941

T-34 MEDIUM TANK

"Numerous Russian T-34s went into action and inflicted heavy losses on the German tanks at Mzensk in 1941. Up to that time we had enjoyed tank superiority, but from now on the situation was reversed. The prospect of rapid, decisive victories was fading in consequence." So wrote German General Heinz Guderian, one of the world's foremost experts on armoured warfare, in his post-Second World War book *Panzer Leader*.

Guderian realised that the introduction of the Soviet T-34 medium tank on the Eastern Front meant that for the first time a Red Army tank approached the combat performance of contemporary German tanks, which had previously dominated the battlefield. While the T-34 made its combat debut in November 1941, a new design to replace the older T-26 and BT series tanks had been in the works since 1937. Engineer Mikhail Koshkin was charged with leading a team to design a new generation of tanks at the Kharkiv Komintern Locomotive plant in Ukraine.

By 1940, the T-34 prototype, designated the A-20, had been developed, but lessons had been learned during brief battles with the Japanese along the Manchurian border, otherwise known as the Battles of Khalkhin Gol (May-September 1939). The experience on the ground in these battles called into serious question several aspects of the performance of existing Soviet tanks. A second prototype, the A-32, was developed, incorporating these lessons. Koshkin had been individually working with new concepts for a medium tank since 1934 and decided to name the ensuing production model T-34 in a nod to the long trek towards a viable combat design.

The T-34 medium tank finally entered mass production in 1940, but combat experience resulted in modifications to the original design. This included a more powerful main weapon, upgraded from 76.2mm to 85mm, additional armour, and a turret that accommodated three crewmen rather than two. The Germans realised rapidly that the T-34 outclassed their existing frontline tanks, contributing to a surge in German redesign as well.

"THE GERMANS REALISED RAPIDLY THAT THE T-34 OUTCLASSED THEIR EXISTING FRONTLINE TANKS"

T-34 MEDIUM TANK

COMMISSIONED:	1937
ORIGIN:	SOVIET UNION
LENGTH:	6 METRES
RANGE:	300 KILOMETRES
ENGINE:	12-CYLINDER V-2-34 WATER-COOLED DIESEL
CREW:	4
PRIMARY WEAPON:	76.2MM L-11 OR 76.2MM F-34; LATER ZIS-S-53 85MM CANNON
SECONDARY WEAPON:	2X 7.62MM DT MACHINE GUNS

ENGINE

The 12-cylinder V-2-34 water-cooled diesel engine generated 500 horsepower and produced a top speed of 55 kilometres per hour. The engine was designed at the Kharkiv Locomotive Factory and was in high demand for numerous Red Army armoured vehicles. Its hull mounts, clutch and other features were modified from the BT series for the T-34. An early shortage of the V-2-34 engine compelled manufacturers to fit the first T-34s with the MT-17 petrol engine, an adaptation of the license-built German BMW VI piston engine originally designed for aircraft, which was already in standard usage with earlier Soviet medium and light tanks.

ARMAMENT

The T-34 was originally armed with the L-11 76.2mm cannon. This was subsequently upgraded to the 76.2mm L-34, which provided greater muzzle velocity and penetrating power against German armour.

Although the L-34 was capable of penetrating the armour of early German tanks at moderate distances, a new generation of enemy tanks with thicker armour was introduced as the war on the Eastern Front wore on. In response the Soviets installed the ZiS-S-53 85mm cannon, with even greater firepower in a reconfigured turret, and the T-34/85 entered production in 1944. A pair of 7.62mm DT machine guns were mounted in the turret and hull for protection against infantry and anti-tank weapons.

The forward-facing hull-mounted machine gun next to the driver's hatch

A Soviet tank commander strikes a resolute pose beside his crewmen. The T-34 was engineered with little attention to the comfort of the crew

DESIGN

The design of the 26.5-tonne T-34 medium tank emanated from the earlier BT series and began taking shape in the mid-1930s. Its distinctive squat silhouette offered a minimal target to enemy gunners, and sloped armour up to 52mm thick provided enhanced protection. The Christie coil spring suspension was actually engineered by American Walter Christie and rejected by the US Army. Initially, the T-34 was equipped with rubber road wheels, but material shortages resulted in later production vehicles utilising steel rims. With the introduction of the T-34/85, electrical turret traverse and an upgraded transmission enhanced performance, along with the more powerful main weapon.

Far right: Painted in white camouflage against a winter landscape, T-34s line up as far as the eye can see
Right: The T-34's simple design made it quick and cheap to manufacture, relative to its German counterparts

T-34 MEDIUM TANK

"THE FOUR-MAN CREW INCLUDED THE COMMANDER, TURRET GUNNER, DRIVER, AND BOW MACHINE GUNNER"

CREW COMPARTMENT

The early T-34 interior was cramped and poorly designed. The four-man crew included the commander, turret gunner, driver and bow machine gunner. Ergonomically, the two-man turret configuration required the commander to load the main weapon, reducing the tank's combat efficiency, as did the lack of a turret basket. The driver sat forwards in the hull on the left and operated the T-34 with tillers. By the spring of 1944, the redesigned T-34/85 was introduced with a three-man turret based on that of the KV-85 series of heavy tanks and the addition of a fifth crewman to load the 85mm cannon.

ALLIED INVASION OF ITALY

ALLIED INVASION OF ITALY

3 September 1943

After the successful invasion of Sicily in July 1943, the Allies turned their attention to the Italian mainland in order to gain a larger foothold in Southern Europe and push back German forces and the remnants of the Italian Army after the fall of Mussolini's regime on 25 July. The invasion of Italy would comprise three separate landings made by British, Canadian and American troops. Operation Avalanche would be the largest of the landings taking place at Salerno. A combined American and British force would land on the beaches at Salerno, with support from the Royal Navy and U.S Navy.

KEY BATTLE

PROKHOROVKA
AND THE FIGHT FOR HILL 252.2

On 12 July 1943, with victory in the Battle of Kursk hanging in the balance, one devastating armoured clash on the German southern pincer proved decisive

WORDS **DR BEN WHEATLEY**

Six days after the Germans launched Operation Citadel, which threatened to surround and cut off several Red Army divisions of the Central and Voronezh Fronts, German panzers continued to make progress, with the II-SS Panzer Corps moving in on the city of Prokhorovka.

At 08:50 on 11 July the German Leibstandarte SS Panzergrenadier Division overcame an anti-tank ditch that was to play a key role. SS War Correspondent Johan King's photos confirm the road bridge over this obstacle was captured intact. Beyond the anti-tank ditch stretched Hill 252.2 "like an enormous wave" – the Germans were 1.6 miles (2.5km) from Prokhorovka.

The Soviet 9th Guards Paratroop Division put up a fierce defence of the heights, which delayed the German advance and forced the Leibstandarte to deploy its SPW (armoured personnel carrier) battalion (2nd SS Panzergrenadier Regiment III Battalion), panzer battalion and Sf Grille (self-propelled heavy infantry guns) to complete the capture of Hill 252.2 and the hilltop Oktiabrskiy state farm.

The heights were finally captured by the Leibstandarte at 14:10. The Leibstandarte's SPW battalion and Sf Grille would later embark on a probing attack in the direction of Prokhorovka. However, beyond Hill 252.2 the Germans came under intense Soviet bombardment, as a result of which the SPW battalion only managed to advance a short distance before having to retreat to its start lines. (King's photographs captured some of the fighting for Hill 252.2).

On 12 July the Leibstandarte's units remained widely dispersed. On the right wing, south of the railway embankment, stood 1st SS Panzergrenadier Regiment, and on the left, far forward in the wake of Hill 252.2, 2nd SS Panzergrenadier Regiment. The division's panzer regiment, on the other hand, was recovering from its exertions of the previous day behind Hill 252.2 and the anti-tank ditch. At this time the Leibstandarte's panzer regiment consisted of just one panzer battalion (its II) with three companies (47 operational Panzer IVs – it began Operation Citadel with 79 operational Pz IVs), to which a heavy panzer company had been attached (four operational Panzer VIs – Tiger tanks – the company began Operation Citadel with 12 operational Tigers). The panzer regiment's other

Even on 11 July the Leibstandarte faced numerous Soviet armoured counter attacks on Hill 252. Here a Leibstandarte Pz IV on Hill 252.2 scans the landscape for Soviet armour

PROKHOROVKA

battalion (its I) was back in Germany undergoing conversion to the Panther tank. Therefore, on 12 July between the railway embankment and the River Psel two full-strength tank brigades of the 5th Guards Tank Army would face a single reinforced panzer battalion.

When Soviet General Pavel Rotmistrov launched the attack on the morning of 12 July from the brick factory 0.6 miles (1km) north-west of Prokhorovka, many of the Leibstandarte's exhausted troops were still asleep; this was made possible as the Soviets chose to launch their attack without a preparatory artillery barrage, as was usual. The foremost German unit at that moment was once again the 2nd SS Panzergrenadier Regiment's III (SPW) Battalion.

At 09:15, on the morning of 12 July, the following scene was described by an SS soldier on Hill 252.2: "We were all fast asleep when they were suddenly all over us with aircraft and an endless mass of tanks with infantry riding on them. It was hell. They were around us, over us, among us. We fought man to man."

"IT WAS HELL. THEY WERE AROUND US, OVER US, AMONG US. WE FOUGHT MAN TO MAN"

The first German panzer officer to see this Soviet tank avalanche was SS Obersturmführer Rudolf von Ribbentrop, the commander of the Leibstandarte panzer battalion's 6th company. Looking up at Hill 252.2 that morning he saw violet signal flares, meaning 'tank alarm'. The signals were "seen all along the crest of the slope" and also appeared "farther to the right at the railway embankment". While the other two panzer companies remained behind the anti-tank ditch, Ribbentrop, in Panzer IV '605', set off up the hill along with his company's other six operational Panzer IVs…

"On reaching the crest of the slope we saw another low rise about 200 metres away on the other side of a small valley, on which our infantry positions were obviously located… The small valley extended to our left, and as we drove down the forward slope we spotted the first T-34s which were apparently attempting to outflank us from the left. We halted on the slope and opened fire, hitting several of the enemy. A number of Russian tanks were left burning. For a good gunner 800 metres was the ideal range."

Ribbentrop then saw a huge column of tanks approaching: "As we waited to see if further enemy tanks were going to appear, I looked around… about 150 to 200 metres in front of us there emerged from a slight dip in the terrain 15, 20, 30, 40 Russian T-34s, and then too many to count. The wall of tanks rolled towards us. Tank by tank, wave upon wave, an unimaginable mass of armour approaching at top speed." The seven German tanks stood no chance against such overwhelming odds. Two of the leading Panzer IVs were destroyed immediately (unknown tactical numbers), another Panzer IV (most likely '615'), positioned further back on the crest of Hill 252.2, met the same fate soon afterwards, a fourth

A huge explosion looms on the horizon, contributing to the already menacing view of Hill 252.2 from the anti-tank ditch

The Leibstandarte's Sf 150mm heavy infantry guns (Grille), shown here, also participated in the assault on Hill 252.2 which began at 10:30, 11 July

To consolidate its gains at 08:50 the Leibstandarte rapidly sent its armour across the anti-tank ditch and onto the slope of Hill 252.2, 11 July

Pz IV '618' of the Leibstandarte's 6th Panzer Company on Hill 252.2 (11.7.43)

A soldier of the 2nd SS Panzergrenadier Regiment liaises with a crew member from the Leibstandarte 5th Panzer Company

Panzer IV was severely damaged and immobilised (probably '616'). The other three Panzer IVs ('605', '618' and '625') managed to survive the encounter unscathed.

The attacking formation which appeared so suddenly was the mass of 29th Tank Corps, led by Major General Kirichenko, consisting of 228 operational AFVs. The attack at this location was carried out by 31st and 32nd Tank Brigades and 53rd Motorised Rifle Brigade, supported by a self-propelled gun regiment and 26th Guards Paratroop Regiment. Once the Soviet tanks had passed the crest of Hill 252.2, they raced down the incline towards the two German panzer companies, which opened fire on them from behind the anti-tank ditch.

Mistaking the German Panzer IVs for Tiger tanks, the Soviet tankers wanted to eliminate their range superiority as quickly as possible. If the armada of Soviet tanks broke through in depth, as must have initially seemed likely, it could only result in the collapse of the German front. Then, in a few minutes, everything changed.

Due to an incredible oversight the Soviets had overlooked the anti-tank ditch. The obstacle had been dug by Soviet infantry and stretched across the base of Hill 252.2 at right angles to the German – now Soviet – direction of attack. According to German testimony "more and more

> **"THE TWO COMPANIES OF PANZER IVS WOULD NORMALLY HAVE STOOD NO CHANCE OF STOPPING THE SOVIET AVALANCHE OF STEEL. HOWEVER, NOW IT WAS SIMPLY 'TARGET PRACTICE AT MOVING TARGETS'"**

T-34s came over the crest, raced down the slope and overturned in the anti-tank ditch behind which we were positioned". German testimony even spoke of tanks attempting to hurdle the anti-tank ditch. How many Soviet tanks actually crashed into the anti-tank ditch is a moot point, but there is no doubt the presence of the obstacle was either directly or indirectly the chief cause of the 29th Tank Corps' armoured difficulties.

Ribbentrop's Panzer IV '605' and '618' had managed to get away by moving alongside the Soviet tanks in a thick cloud of dust. Ribbentrop's other remaining operational Panzer IV, '625', is said to have stayed on the battlefield (close to the railway embankment) with a lowered and temporarily jammed main gun. Ribbentrop recalled: "Now the T-34s recognised the ditch and tried to veer left to the road in order to get across the ditch via the bridge, which had been repaired [King's photographic evidence from 11 July 1943 clearly shows that the bridge had been captured intact]. What happened then is indescribable… as they converged on the bridge, the Russians were exposed on the flanks and made easier targets. Burning T-34s ran into and over each other. An inferno of fire, smoke, burning tanks, dead and wounded!" On the other side of the anti-tank ditch the two companies of Panzer IVs would normally have stood no chance of stopping the Soviet avalanche of steel. However, now it was simply "target practice at moving targets".

By noon the Leibstandarte's 2nd SS Panzergrenadier Regiment had recaptured Hill 252.2 and the Oktiabrskiy state farm. According to Valeriy Zamulin's most recent estimate, on 12 July the Soviet 29th Tank Corps alone lost 102 tanks and assault guns as write-offs (60 T-34s, 31 T-70s, eight SU-122s, three SU-76s). After reviewing the available Soviet records, it is the author's calculation that between 12 and 16 July the 29th Tank Corps lost 132 of its 250 tanks and assault guns as write-offs (83 T-34s, 37 T-70s, one KV-1, eight SU-122s, three SU-76s). The vast majority of these losses unquestionably would have occurred on 12 July.

In addition to Luftwaffe pictures of the battlefield we are extremely fortunate to have remarkable post-battle pictures taken from a Soviet aircraft flying low over the Prokhorovka battlefield. These pictures were kindly passed to the author by Valeriy Zamulin and can be found in his excellent 2015 book *The Battle of Kursk 1943: The View through the Camera Lens*.

In the foreground of one the images we can clearly see a destroyed Leibstandarte Panzer IV. The tank was lost just behind the diagonal running dirt track that stretches from the Belgorod-Prokhorovka road/railway crossing to the Oktiabrskiy state farm. Close by, a destroyed Soviet T-34 is seen behind an infantry trench. This site is just on the crest of Hill 252.2 and can easily be found in the Luftwaffe pictures of 16 July and 7 August.

Wrecks from the 29th Tank Corps are circled in red in the fields in front of the anti-tank ditch in this Luftwaffe reconnaissance photo, 7 August 1943

A Soviet aircraft flying low over the Prokhorovka battlefield photographed the aftermath of the engagement (destroyed tanks circled in red)

In the foreground a destroyed Leibstandarte Panzer IV is circled in black; circled in red is a wrecked Soviet T-34 behind an infantry trench

Given that the Panzer IV is located close to Hill 252.2's crest (from the Germans' point of view) it is likely that this Panzer IV saw combat slightly later than Ribbentrop's leading panzers and as a result it was probably the third and final Leibstandarte Panzer IV lost on the morning of 12 July. It is also likely that the destroyed Panzer IV was '615', commanded by Obersturmführer Malchow. According to the testimony of '615's loader, Walter Kettle, the tank was hit, caught fire and after being abandoned exploded. Kettle implies that his tank (unlike the lead Panzer IVs) did not open fire on the first group of Soviet tanks that had attempted to outflank Ribbentrop's leading tanks.

Kettle stated that Malchow instead merely counted the flanking Soviet tanks through his binoculars. Clearly, Malchow's tank was not among the lead Panzer IVs that day; if '615' had been at the forefront of the action on 12 July then it would have also engaged the flanking Soviet tanks. This raises the probability that the destroyed Panzer IV captured on camera by the low-flying Soviet aircraft was indeed Panzer IV '615'; its location away from the undulating terrain (the first point of engagement) mentioned by Ribbentrop supports this view.

Another photo from the Soviet flight was taken slightly closer to the parallel road that separates the two fields in front of the anti-tank ditch; a destroyed Leibstandarte SPW is particularly prominent on the right of the picture. The destruction caused to the 29th Tank Corps armour in the fields in front of the anti-tank ditch is clearly visible in these photographs (the author has highlighted some of the more obvious wrecks in a 7 August Luftwaffe reconnaissance picture, p29). Later armoured wrecks from across the battlefield were dragged to a railway spur on the outskirts of Prokhorovka (images of this railway spur, with over 100 armoured wrecks visible, can be found in the author's new book The Panzers of Prokhorovka).

The disproportionally high number of Soviet armoured losses (as many as 246 AFV during the battle and its immediate aftermath) did not, however, equate to a Soviet defeat at Prokhorovka. On two occasions (11 and 13 July) the German attackers simply had no answer to the extremely powerful Soviet defences that had been installed to protect Prokhorovka. These defences included a formidable artillery capability and an impenetrable anti-tank screen. The Soviets also maintained a high number of operational tanks; even after the battle the 5th Guards Tank Army still possessed over 650 AFV. As a result of these realities the Germans, having failed to obtain flanking support, had no hope of continuing their advance on the Prokhorovka axis. Even though this victory may not be the one of legend, the Soviet soldiers who fought so courageously against Nazism at Prokhorovka still deserve our deepest respect and gratitude for their victory.

THE PANZERS OF PROKHOROVKA

Dr Ben Wheatley's book, lifting the lid on some of the biggest myths and misconceptions at the epicentre of the Battle of Kursk, is available now from Osprey Publishing.

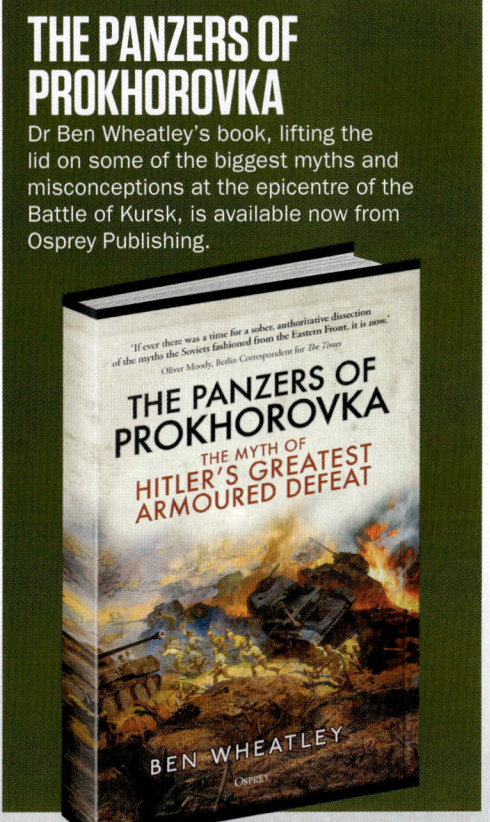

★ 28 NOVEMBER 1943 ★

THE TEHRAN CONFERENCE

The first meeting of Roosevelt, Churchill and Stalin solidified an unlikely alliance

WORDS JAMES HORTON

In 1935, the country known as Persia was officially renamed as Iran by its leader Reza Shah, who was eager to mark a new era of independence. However, the outbreak of WWII risked rendering this independence rather short-lived, as both the Allied and Axis forces eyed Iran as a useful territory to occupy.

The Shah declared neutrality, but in private he favoured the Axis powers. Iran relied heavily on trade with Germany and the country had been occupied by British and Soviet forces in the previous war, an event the Shah had no interest in allowing to be repeated. Therefore, despite Hitler's offensive rhetoric about the inferiority of non-Europeans, the Shah's scepticism of the Allies kept them at arm's reach. He was right to be suspicious, because towards the end of 1941 he was forcibly deposed from his throne in favour of his Anglophile son. By September 1943, Iran had declared war on Germany, Allied forces had moved in, and the country was being used as a conduit for the British and US to supply the Soviet Union. Then, on 28 November 1943, Iran became one of the most defining centres for the war. Not because armies clashed within its borders, but because the three mightiest powers of the Allies converged there for a summit that would seal their joint campaign against the Axis powers.

The war had been raging in Europe since 1939, and the British, Americans and Soviets had been embroiled in an allied conflict with Hitler's Germany for nearly two years. Yet neither Prime Minister Winston Churchill nor President Franklin D. Roosevelt had ever met Soviet General Secretary Joseph Stalin. Churchill and Roosevelt were reluctant allies with the Soviets, thrust together by their mutual enemy of the Axis powers.

But the 'Big Three' powers were in an apt position to meet when they did. The tide had slowly been turning against the Germans, who had faced serious reversals in their invasion of the Soviet Union, and had been bullied out of Africa by the British and American forces. The three leaders felt it was time to meet in person to not only solidify their war effort and bring the conflict to a victorious conclusion, but also to discuss the fates of the soon-to-be liberated territories held by the Axis forces.

General Secretary Joseph Stalin, President Franklin D. Roosevelt and Prime Minister Winston Churchill at the Tehran Conference

Stalin arrived at the conference primarily concerned with the Germans, who had invaded his territory, attempted to capture his capital, and until recently had seized much of the Caucasus. The Soviet Union was at that time the only Allied power waging a land war against Germany on European soil, and Stalin wanted his Western comrades to open a new front on Hitler's other flank. But Stalin's ambitions did not end there; he also had a strong interest in the fates of his neighbouring states in Eastern Europe. Stalin was aware that his Western allies may prove to be only temporary, and therefore he wanted to wed them to concessions while they still needed his army.

Roosevelt arrived with an agenda that was equally concerned with the other major Axis power, Japan. He wanted the Soviets to commit to the Eastern theatre and engage with the Japanese towards the Pacific. Churchill, for his part, was keen on a joint Anglo-American land invasion into northwestern mainland Europe. But he also wanted to invest resources into opening a Mediterranean theatre of war that attacked north through Italy.

> "HE ALSO WANTED TO INVEST RESOURCES INTO OPENING A MEDITERRANEAN THEATRE OF WAR THAT ATTACKED NORTH THROUGH ITALY"

The summit took place with jovial interactions between the leaders and their advisors, with Churchill keen to impress with his wit and Roosevelt eager to accommodate. Such was the charm offensive from the Western allies that Churchill gifted Stalin, on behalf of King George VI, a ceremonial longsword – the Sword of Stalingrad – made for the 'Man of Steel' himself. But these friendly interactions did not distract Stalin from his agenda. He was recorded as being forceful and calculating throughout the talks and emerged the clear winner after successfully dividing the other two leaders.

Churchill's second theatre in the Mediterranean was flatly refused by Stalin, who received backing on this account from Roosevelt. Correctly sensing that the US leader would acquiesce to his more audacious terms, the Soviet leader also secured acceptance that following the war Poland would become a Soviet 'client state'. Soviet borders would also expand into Poland, and in return Poland's borders would extend into Germany.

However, all three leaders left with their major aims achieved. The most notable of these agreements was that Britain and the US would invade France by May the following year from both the north and south. In return, Stalin would draw forces away from the invasion points by launching major offensives on the Eastern Front. Stalin also agreed to join the war against Japan once Germany had been defeated.

The three leaders left the summit on 1 December aware that they'd enjoyed different degrees of success. Stalin was likely the winner, but the agreements between the three at least ensured that the Axis powers would be the ones who ultimately lost.

American soldiers disembark from a landing craft during training exercises for Operation Overlord, which was agreed during the Tehran conference

KEY EVENT

THE LIBERATION OF ROME

After a long, hard campaign up the peninsula, the Allies liberated the Eternal City just days before the invasion of occupied France began

WORDS **JOHN BEALES**

When the North African campaign turned decisively in the Allies' favour in 1942, it was a significant boost to morale and plans were immediately made to invade Italy and thereby neutralise Nazi Germany's junior fascist partner. However, the Allies were split between prioritising the planned invasion of Europe in the west or grinding down Axis resistance in Italy to make the larger invasion easier.

The latter idea prevailed but the Italian campaign literally became a bloody uphill struggle, with Monte Cassino being the clearest example. In the aftermath of the battle there was a chance to thrust into the German line of retreat. In a costly example of tense Allied relations, the British General Alexander ordered the US Fifth Army under General Mark Clark to cut off the German retreat from the Cassino area. However, Clark disobeyed his superior and decided to enter Rome instead.

American forces triumphantly entered the capital on 4-5 June 1944, but by doing this Clark had also let the threatened German 10th Army escape. His decision has been described by historian Carlo D'Este "as militarily stupid as it was insubordinate." Not only did D-Day overshadow the liberation only 24 hours later, but also the Germans managed to withdraw to tough defences at the Gothic Line.

This impeded Allied progress and further bloodshed ensued. British veteran of the Italian campaign Theo Davies, who was still fighting at the time of the liberation, later reflected on Clark's decision: "If he'd turned and cut the Germans off he would have bagged a few divisions of them. It wouldn't have ended the war but it would have put a lot more pressure on the Germans and they would have had to bring in more replacements. At the time the thinking was that everybody thought it was a big mistake."

THE BATTLE FOR EUROPE
1944

The Summer of 1944 saw the Western Allies launch their major invasion of occupied France, while the campaign in mainland Italy gathered pace. In the East, the Red Army began a series of immense counterattacks, crippling Axis forces and pushing them back to the border of the Reich. Meanwhile in the Pacific, the Allied island-hopping campaign reached the Philippines, freeing the archipelago from Japanese occupation.

THE LIBERATION OF ROME

Allied vehicles and troops pictured outside the Vittorio Emmanuel memorial and the Piazza Venezia in Rome, 10 June 1944

★ KEY BATTLE ★

MONTE CASSINO
Q&A: JAMES HOLLAND

The renowned author, historian and broadcaster explains why the offensive in the Italian mountains was so costly for the Allies, and how his new research has changed his view of the gruelling battles for the Gustav Line

WORDS **LOUIS HARDIMAN**

Monte Cassino town burns after an Allied bombardment

MONTE CASSINO

Allied troops march through the ruins of Monte Cassino town

T he hardest-fought battle in Italy during the Second World War came in the winter and spring of 1944 as the previously unstoppable Allied advance on Rome came up against the Gustav Line. Threading coast-to-coast through the Apennine Mountains, it was a formidable defensive barrier formed of minefields, bunkers and booby traps. Perched at its strongest point was the Monastery at Monte Cassino.

In his book *Cassino '44*, James Holland draws from diaries, letters and other contemporary sources from those on the frontline. Here he recounts the story of the attack on Monte Cassino, sharing what he learned from delving into the source material.

Polish 2nd Corps soldiers throw grenades at the enemy in Monte Cassino

What was Monte Cassino's significance and why was it so hard to capture?
Monte Cassino itself is the mountain overlooking Cassino town. Highway 6, the old Via Casilina, runs directly underneath Cassino and then to Rome. There were four major roads from the south to the north that all converged on the capital. One is on the western coast and it was narrow, with mountain passes and little room for manoeuvre. There was one on the Adriatic Coast which crossed the Appenine Mountains. Another was in the middle, also through the mountains, winding and easy to defend. The only prominent artery north was the Via Casilina. Although you might think the Allies were mechanised with enough tanks to do what they liked, they needed these main roads to move North.

The problem was that any Germans on the top of Monte Cassino overlooked Via Casilina and could direct pre-arranged artillery fire on anyone trying to use that road. Until they had cleared the enemy observers from the mountains, the Allies had a problem.

The Germans knew that the observers were vulnerable and protected them with lots of infantry that the Allies had to clear. However, it was difficult to attack as that would mean exposing themselves. Meanwhile, the defenders could hide

"UNTIL THEY HAD CLEARED THE ENEMY OBSERVERS FROM THE MOUNTAINS, THE ALLIES HAD A PROBLEM"

behind rocks or in fissures. That's why Monte Cassino became the crux of the whole defensive position that ran across the narrow peninsula of Italy. It was the strongest point.

What situation did Lieutenant General Sir Bernard Freyberg inherit when he was made commander of the New Zealand Corps?
I greatly respect Freyberg as a soldier but not much as a commander. The problem was that the American 34th 'Red Bulls' Infantry Division had gone up from the beginning of January and early February and taken two-thirds of the Monte Cassino massif. They couldn't get it over the line because they didn't understand the defensive structure that the Germans had created.

The Germans had figure-of-eight defences around Point 593 and the Americans had to overwhelm more than 50 percent of two of the circles of the figure-of-eight simultaneously. They didn't know they had to do that. The Red Bulls thought they were close because they could see

The Monte Cassino monastery was destroyed by Allied bombardment

CASSINO '44 BY JAMES HOLLAND IS AVAILABLE NOW

the Liri Valley beyond with the Via Casilina running through. That made them think it just needed one more push.

When the New Zealand Corps was created, Allied command was hoping they could exploit this success. The problem was that when suddenly creating an extra corps, bringing three divisions over from the British Eighth Army on the Adriatic Coast to join the American Fifth Army, they had to make the most senior general the corps commander. The most senior and only lieutenant general available was Freyberg, a New Zealander.

The problem was that he had been over-promoted and was not up to it. The New Zealanders were also massively punching above their weight in the Second World War. They were a small country with a tiny population but offered a lot in terms of aircrew and soldiers in North Africa, Syria and now Italy. There was a mutiny back at home, so Freyberg had to move carefully.

Attached to Freyberg was the superb 4th Indian Division led by Francis Tuker. However, Tuker got rheumatoid arthritis at the wrong moment because he came up with a much better plan than the bombing of the abbey. Tuker wanted to go further up the massif towards Monte Cairo. His argument was that although it was higher, the ground was more open compared to the Cassino town end of the massif, which was riven with fissures and chasms.

The Allies could only put down a company of 100 men at a time on the narrow ridges, not enough to overwhelm the enemy. The smoothed-out landscape at Monte Cairo allowed for an attack on a broader front. The most robust German defences were also at the end of the massif, not further to the north.

> "IT'S A HEARTBREAKING STORY THAT WAS MADE WORSE BY THE FACT THAT ONE OF THE GREATEST ARTISTIC TREASURES OF EUROPE WAS DESTROYED IN THE PROCESS, COMPLETELY NEEDLESSLY"

Why did Freyberg bomb the monastery?
Tuker suggested the attack at Monte Cairo and Freyberg was all for it. Then Freyberg got ill and decided to go with what the Americans suggested, which was to continue the Red Bulls' attack at the end of the Monte Cassino massif.

Tuker argued that the only way to do that properly was to smother the entire Monte Cassino massif with heavy general-purpose bombs: 4,000lb (1,800kg) and 2,500lb (1,100kg) bombs, whereas 1,000lb (450kg) or 500lb (230kg) bombs wouldn't cut it. The Allies had to destroy everything, covering the whole site, followed by an immediate infantry attack. That was a difficult operation, involving the destruction of the abbey.

Tuker was still arguing for his suggestion, but if Freyberg was going to insist on the American plan, these were the consequences.

Tuker went back to hospital and Freyberg did the opposite of what he had asked. Freyberg used 'Kitty' bombers to attack the monastery. It's hard to understand how Freyberg got this the wrong way around. General Mark W Clark, Fifth Army commander, was also appalled by the idea. He complained to General Harold Alexander, the Army Group commander, who told Clark that he must support whatever Freyberg said he needed. The net result was an absolute fiasco because they didn't attack with large general-purpose bombs and the main target was the abbey rather than spreading their ordnance. As far as we can tell, not a single German was killed. There was also no co-ordination with the infantry, who weren't told the bombing was going to happen.

The bombing of the abbey was one of those moments that didn't affect the result of the war, but it certainly affected the campaign's outcome. It was entirely because Freyberg had been given a command that was beyond his ken.

Which German units were defending Monte Cassino against the Allied attacks?
When Monte Cassino was first attacked, members of the German 44th Infantry Division defended it. They were badly overstretched, mauled and in no state to resist. The 90th Panzergrenadier and 1st Fallschirmjäger parachute troops arrived soon after. These units were weakened and understrength, with many teenagers, but also a cadre of experienced men, NCOs and junior

officers that had been through the blitzkrieg, the Eastern Front and Crete. They were very successful at digging in, making use of the ground and not letting go of their [defences].

The interesting thing about the 1st Fallschirmjäger Division was that they were not the best-trained and you would hardly call them elite forces. However, they were all German volunteers, disciplined and motivated. That made a huge difference, particularly in defence. The shortfall in training among the junior ranks was made up by the hard core of experience and the fact they were fanatical and in tune with the regime. Even just being German was more than could be said for the Czech and Poles in German uniforms, who didn't want to be there.

What new difficulties did the Allies face when trying to make their final attack on the Monte Cassino massif?
The big problem was that the last bit of the Monte Cassino massif tapers into a triangle and it's cut across with ridgelines, not too dissimilar from the WiFi symbol. The problem with the ridgelines, particularly the main Snakeshead ridge that culminated in Point 593, was that they weren't wide and had little room for manoeuvre. The Allies could have a whole regiment or brigade up there, but they couldn't put 1,500 or 2,000 men in at a time as there wasn't the space to cope with them. It was like going into a meat grinder and attacking troops were chewed up because of the exposure of the open rock with nowhere to run or hide. There would be mortars, grenades and shells coming in, creating splinters of rock flying.

The Sussex Battalion, part of the 5th Indian Infantry Division, was attacking and were told that the Americans had been unable to capture Point 593, which they had to clear before the main attack could go in. This was the evening after the bombing of the monastery, which stopped the main attack from coming immediately after.

They failed at taking Point 593 and tried again the following night, but it would always be the same problem. Until the Allies understood the nature of the defences, it didn't matter how many companies they fed in – they'd get the same result when they hit the wall of machine guns, mortars and grenades. It was not until May that the Poles

Two Red Cross nurses observe the early stages of the bombardment

were up there and finally understood how the defensive system worked. Now, they could do something about it.

What does the source material tell us about the difficulties the Allies experienced in urban warfare in Cassino town?
The main problem was that Alexander decided to wait until the land dried out and they could bring to bear their considerable advantages in air power, mechanisation and materiel. That was sensible, but there was a case for having a limited operation to clear Cassino town as a jump-off point. Alexander insisted that they didn't do anything until they had three clear-weather days. All the troops for the attack on Cassino town were brought up in the last week of February, but it was not until the middle of March that the weather was good enough to launch the attack.

Even so, the attack should have been a complete cakewalk. The Allies planned to bomb the town and pulverise it completely, which sounds incredibly wanton and as bad as destroying the abbey, but it was not. As we have seen [many times], fighting in a built-up area is incredibly difficult, as attacking troops can't see far ahead. Destroying the buildings creates piles of rubble, but they could at least see ahead of themselves.

Having flattened the town, the Allies needed to overwhelm it in two places with vast numbers of troops, but Freyberg didn't do it. He sent in a battalion with a couple of companies, and again, it was too little. The Germans reinforced the remains of the town overnight. The New Zealanders managed to take two-thirds of the town, but not the last third that really counted.

Who were the first Allied soldiers to enter the monastery itself?
It was the Poles that finally entered the monastery and they hadn't been there very long. They had only moved up at the very end of April, ready for launching the attack on Monte Cassino, which they did in the early hours of 12 May. From their point of view, there was a great pride that they had been able to do what no one else had managed so far. Most Polish troops were Catholic and the Benedictine order that the Monte Cassino monks followed was also Catholic. Upon entering the monastery, there was [mixed emotions].

The story of the 2nd Polish Corps was just extraordinary because most of the men had been captured by the Soviets at the start of the war in 1939 and then transported to the gulags. They were only released from the Soviet Union after a deal was made after Operation Barbarossa. Suddenly, the Western Allies were on the same side as the Soviet Union and Winston Churchill promised to train the Polish prisoners and get them fighting.

The new Polish units had to go from their gulags in the Arctic Circle down to Uzbekistan, where they were mustering under General Władysław Anders. By this point, most of them were emaciated and ill, struggling with malaria, typhus, typhoid and a host of other nasties. The survivors were then transferred from Uzbekistan into Iran and then Kirkuk, northern Iraq, where they trained. Having built up their strength, they travelled to Palestine and then, in late 1943 and early 1944, to Italy. Their first proper action was the assault on Monte Cassino in May 1944.

Freyberg (centre) clambers among the ruins of Monte Cassino monastery with New Zealand's Prime Minister Peter Fraser

Mussolini's popularity declined rapidly as the Allies advanced up the Italian mainland

KEY EVENT

MUSSOLINI'S DOWNFALL

Once the most powerful man in Italy, Il Duce met his end fleeing his country in disguise as the war drew to its bitter end

WORDS **DAVID SMITH**

MUSSOLINI'S DOWNFALL

Italian partisans, aligned with the Action Party, patrol the streets of Milan after the city's liberation

The hunched figure in the back of the German truck might not have merited a second glance had he not conspicuously been wearing sunglasses. The Luftwaffe corporal, resting his chin on the sub-machine gun between his knees, was certainly not what the partisans of the 52nd Garibaldi Brigade were looking for. They were intent only on finding any fugitive Italians within the small column of German troops.

However, the sunglasses – worn on a cloudy day – attracted attention and a closer examination of the German corporal revealed the unmistakable features of Benito Amilcare Andrea Mussolini, former Prime Minister and dictator of Italy. It was 27 April 1945, and the story of 'Il Duce' ('the leader'), was coming to its conclusion.

The slow defeat

On 29 July 1943, the day of his 60th birthday, Il Duce was in captivity on the island of Ponza, before being moved to an impressive suite at the Hotel Campo Imperatore, 1,800 metres up the Gran Sasso mountain in the Apennines

By this stage in the conflict, nobody on either side had any doubts that Italy would try to extricate itself from the war. The critical factor in the tragic events that followed would be the German ability to act on that realisation.

While the Allies bogged themselves down in negotiations with the new government – led by Marshal Pietro Badoglio – over the terms of an Italian surrender, the Germans were already quietly moving troops into Italy.

When the inevitable armistice between Italy and the Allies was announced, the Germans were ready with Operation Achse, which saw German troops replace Italians in southern France, the Balkans and the Aegean. They also immediately disarmed more than half a million Italian troops in their native country – a staggering 56 divisions of the Italian Army were simply dismantled.

On 12 September, 12 gliders, carrying over 100 German commandos, were dispatched to 'rescue' Mussolini, who was forced to leave his comfortable hotel in a dangerously overloaded Stork reconnaissance plane. Two days later, he was meeting the Führer.

Hitler offered Mussolini a stark choice – either accept a position at the head of a new Italian government in northern Italy, or face the consequences. "Northern Italy," the Führer warned, "will be forced to envy the fate of Poland if you do not accept to give renewed vigour to the alliance between Germany and Italy, by becoming head of the state and of the new government."

Many Italians had hoped that the armistice with the Allies would mean an end to their war. This was perhaps naïve, but few would have guessed that their struggle was just beginning.

Germany could not allow the Allies to simply occupy a section of Italy and use it as a launch pad for strikes against the Fatherland. The removal of the Italians as a fighting partner, however their abilities were viewed, was nevertheless a major blow and Germany would soon be fighting on three desperately hard fronts as the long-anticipated invasion of Europe neared.

The first Italians to wake up to the reality of the new situation were the soldiers themselves. More than 600,000 became prisoners of war, with the bulk of them shipped to Germany to work as forced labour, while around 200,000 took the alternative of joining the German Army.

Atrocities were common, most notably on the island of Cephalonia, where Italian troops made the mistake of resisting the Germans. More than a thousand were killed in the one-sided fighting that followed, and 5,000 survivors were then systematically massacred.

The Allied offensive from Salerno made slow progress, but had driven the Germans back to a major defensive line by January 1944. Three assaults were launched on the town of Cassino, one of the keystones of the Gustav Line, but the German defences could not be breached. The war had entered a brutal, attritional phase and the Italians found themselves bystanders caught between two destructive forces.

For some, simply standing by and watching was unthinkable, but the understandable desire to do something to respond to the situation would lead Italy into the murky depths of a civil war.

Resistance erupts

Partisan groups had sprung up spontaneously on the declaration of the armistice with the Allies, with an estimated 10,000 civilians arming themselves and forming loosely organised groups. A two-day resistance was also staged at Rome until the Germans threatened to raze the city.

Around 50,000 prisoners of war, mostly from Yugoslavia, were also thrown into the mix when the Italians guarding them simply left their posts. Many headed for the hills and the mountains to join partisan groups.

Such groups were small in number at the start of the war, possibly comprising as few as a dozen men. After the armistice was signed in September 1943, the number of active partisans in Italy would rise sharply.

Following Mussolini's removal, previously banned political parties stepped out of the shadows to form partisan groups with fervent ideological grounding. Almost half of these groups were communists, known as 'Garibaldi Brigades'. The Action Party was the next largest faction, but there were also partisans fighting for the aims of the Socialists, Christian Democrats, Labour Democrats and Liberals, as well as some who spurned any sort of political affiliation at all, such as the Stella Rossa, the 'Red Star Brigade'.

The six major anti-fascist parties organised themselves into the Comitato di Liberazione Nazionale, or Committee of National Liberation (CLN), aiming to co-ordinate resistance to the German occupation and Italian fascist groups. Many of these had sprung up at the same time as Mussolini's new government. Fascist militia, in the form of the Guardia Nazionale Repubblicana (GNR), worked to counter the partisans, aided by the Gestapo, the SS security service, the military-based carabinieri police and fascist gangs.

The situation was seldom clear-cut, with many young men choosing to join an organised unit not

> "MANY ITALIANS HAD HOPED THAT THE ARMISTICE WITH THE ALLIES WOULD MEAN AN END TO THEIR WAR. THIS WAS PERHAPS NAÏVE, BUT FEW WOULD HAVE GUESSED THAT THEIR STRUGGLE WAS JUST BEGINNING"

through any political or ideological conviction, but simply out of desperation and the need for some form of employment. Nevertheless, there were enough fanatics to ensure that fighting between the various factions was often savage.

Historians have long debated the effectiveness of the partisans, but there can be no doubt that they increased the scale of their activities as the Allied Italian campaign progressed. From less than 500 reported attacks in January 1944, there were more than 2,000 in March, which increased to over 3,000 in June.

The attacks, especially when they targeted German soldiers, drew severe retribution. As a rule of thumb the Germans would execute ten prisoners or civilians for every German soldier killed by partisans.

The hamstrung leader

Mussolini despaired at the brutal nature of the German occupation, but his new government was effectively toothless. Based, humiliatingly, at Salò rather than Rome, the Repubblica Sociale Italiana (RSI) saw its various offices scattered over a wide area in a deliberate attempt to limit its ability to function efficiently.

Heaping further humiliation on Il Duce, he was granted a new army of just four divisions, and the bulk of them would need to come from new recruits. Only 12,000 officers and NCOs were allowed to return from Germany and conscription was required to fill out the new army's pitifully meagre ranks. This led to a surge in partisan numbers, as many young men preferred to take their chances in the mountains rather than obey their call-up orders.

Mussolini was not, however, a totally spent force. Falling back on his early career as a journalist, he became a prolific writer once more, churning out propaganda pieces that referred to the Allies as the 'Anglo-American invaders'. He also contrasted their habit of flattening Italian cities and towns with the way the Germans had left Rome intact after being driven out by the American Fifth Army in the June of 1944.

For weeks the Allied military campaign had progressed remorselessly – following success in the fourth Battle of Cassino, in May 1944 – but there had been huge casualties on both sides as the Germans repeatedly fell back on new defensive lines.

The diversion of German units from France to help the Normandy invasion, launched on 6 June (just after the fall of Rome), was the stated aim of the Italian campaign, but as many historians would later note, it was debatable who was tying down whom in the campaign.

Above: Il Duce's control over Italy became absolute in 1925 when he dissolved the democratic government

"PARTISAN GROUPS HAD SPRUNG UP SPONTANEOUSLY ON THE DECLARATION OF THE ARMISTICE WITH THE ALLIES, WITH AN ESTIMATED 10,000 CIVILIANS ARMING THEMSELVES AND FORMING LOOSELY ORGANISED GROUPS"

After executing the fascist leader, Italian partisans hung him, along with his retinue, in one of Milan's public squares

MUSSOLINI'S DOWNFALL

A desperate escape

By the end of 1944, Mussolini was little more than a recluse, but he still had a little fight left in him. He formulated a plan to launch a counteroffensive using his precious four divisions, that failed to make any lasting gains against the allied advance.

In a last display of his old passion, Mussolini gave a speech in Milan in December, drawing rapturous applause from a packed crowd at the Teatro Lirico.

It was little more than a last hurrah. His German doctor declared, in February 1945, that he was the 'victim of a serious physical and moral collapse'. Also crumpling was the German military position, on every front. The Allies broke through the Gothic Line in April, at the same time as they approached Berlin from the West and the Russians approached it from the East.

On 25 April, the partisan leadership met with Mussolini in Milan to work out terms for the surrender of his fascist militia groups. His attempt to work out a deal with them failed, only unconditional surrender to them was acceptable.

Leaving Milan, at 8pm, Mussolini embarked on a desperate bid to escape the country. He made it to Como that night and by 27 April had fallen in with a column of German troops, wearily heading home after their exhausting campaign in Italy.

A partisan roadblock stopped the column and after protracted discussions, the Germans were told they could continue their journey – but that all Italians had to be left behind. The Germans were unconcerned about the fate of their Italian passengers, but did agree to allow Mussolini, and Mussolini alone, to travel with them in disguise. They gave him a greatcoat, helmet, sub-machine gun and the fateful sunglasses, in a futile attempt to obscure the most familiar face in Italy. Recognised quickly when the column was searched, Mussolini was arrested. He had fallen into the hands of the communists in the form of the 52nd Garibaldi Brigade.

The final act

The communists were determined not to hand Mussolini, or the other members of his retinue – including his mistress, Claretta Petacci – over to the Allies. A miserable few hours followed, in which Mussolini's fate was argued over and he was disguised once more, this time by the partisans as they attempted to keep him alive until they had decided what to do with him. The decision, when it came, was brutally simple. Alongside his mistress, Mussolini was riddled with sub-machine gun bullets on 28 April 1945. Although many initially claimed to have been the man to kill Il Duce, confusion still reigns over who actually pulled the trigger.

The remaining members of his retinue were also executed and the bodies, including those of Mussolini and his mistress, were unceremoniously dumped in the Piazzale Loreto in Milan. On the morning of 29 April, the bodies were discovered and a mob quickly gathered to spit, kick and otherwise abuse the corpses. Mussolini, his mistress and others were strung up by their feet, their already stiffened bodies hanging grotesquely. The following day, Hitler committed suicide.

Even then, however, Italy's misery was not over. Mussolini was gone but the partisans had plenty of other targets. An orgy of violence erupted as thousands of fascists, and suspected fascists, were summarily executed.

A young soldier is comforted during an inspection of a paramilitary Black Brigade

Mussolini spent the last two years of his life as a puppet figurehead of the Italian Social Republic

KEY EVENT

D-DAY

On 6 June 1944 Allied forces landed in Normandy by sea and air, beginning the liberation of France and Western Europe

WORDS JAMES HORTON

Allied planning for what would become known as the Battle of Normandy commenced in 1943. It would be given the codename of 'Operation Overlord' and its aim was to establish a large-scale bridgehead on the Continent, from which the Allies would eventually liberate Western Europe from years of German occupation.

Shortly after the German invasion of the Soviet Union in the summer of 1941, Stalin began to push his Western Allies to open a second front in Europe in order to relieve pressure on his own beleaguered forces. Almost a year later, both the United States and the Soviet Union agreed on the urgency to open this second front. However, Churchill persuaded Roosevelt to wait until the Allies were strong enough to mount such a large-scale operation.

Much to Stalin's anger, the Allies instead turned their attention to a series of campaigns in North Africa, the Mediterranean, and the subsequent invasions of Sicily and Italy. Nevertheless, by the middle of 1944, the Western Allies felt ready to launch their long-awaited landings in North-Western Europe.

In addition to the troop and equipment buildup for the coming invasion, the Allies launched an ambitious deception operation codenamed 'Bodyguard'. The Allies knew the Germans would be expecting the invasion, and so they adopted what later proved to be a successful strategy to mislead the Germans as to the time and location of the landings.

The first phase of Overlord would be codenamed 'Operation Neptune', which involved the actual landing of vast numbers of troops, equipment, and supplies along the Normandy coast. What is often referred to today as 'D-Day' remains the largest seaborne invasion in military history. Although the Allies did not achieve all their objectives on D-Day, it paved the way for the eventual liberation of Western Europe.

Images: Getty Images

Omaha beach saw some of the bloodiest fighting on 6 June

SUPREME HEADQUARTERS ALLIED EXPEDITIONARY FORCE

Operation Overlord was led by a group of senior American and British commanders

BERTRAM RAMSAY
Position: Naval Commander In Chief

It took the intervention of Winston Churchill to bring Ramsay back to the Navy after he retired in 1938, and he was put in charge of defending cross-Channel military traffic. He was later in charge of the Dunkirk evacuation and the Normandy invasion.

ARTHUR TEDDER
Position: Deputy Supreme Allied Commander

Tedder was Air Chief Marshall in the RAF when he joined the Supreme Command, Allied Expeditionary Force (SCAEF) in January 1944 as deputy to Eisenhower. He had previously worked with him on the invasion of Sicily and Italy.

DWIGHT D EISENHOWER
Position: Supreme Allied Commander

Eisenhower had made a name for himself as a planner and organiser, rising through the ranks of the US armed services. He was responsible for overseeing and coordinating all of the armed forces involved in Operation Overlord.

BERNARD MONTGOMERY
Position: Ground Forces Commander In Chief

Despite being a divisive figure, Montgomery was nonetheless put in charge of the ground forces for D-Day and Operation Overlord. He planned the overall objectives for American, British and Canadian ground troops in Normandy.

TRAFFORD LEIGH-MALLORY
Position: Air Commander In Chief

Leigh-Mallory joined the planning for Normandy in August 1943. He was in charge of planning bombing raids to disrupt German reinforcement ahead of D-Day, later working in coordination with the army to support ground forces after the invasion.

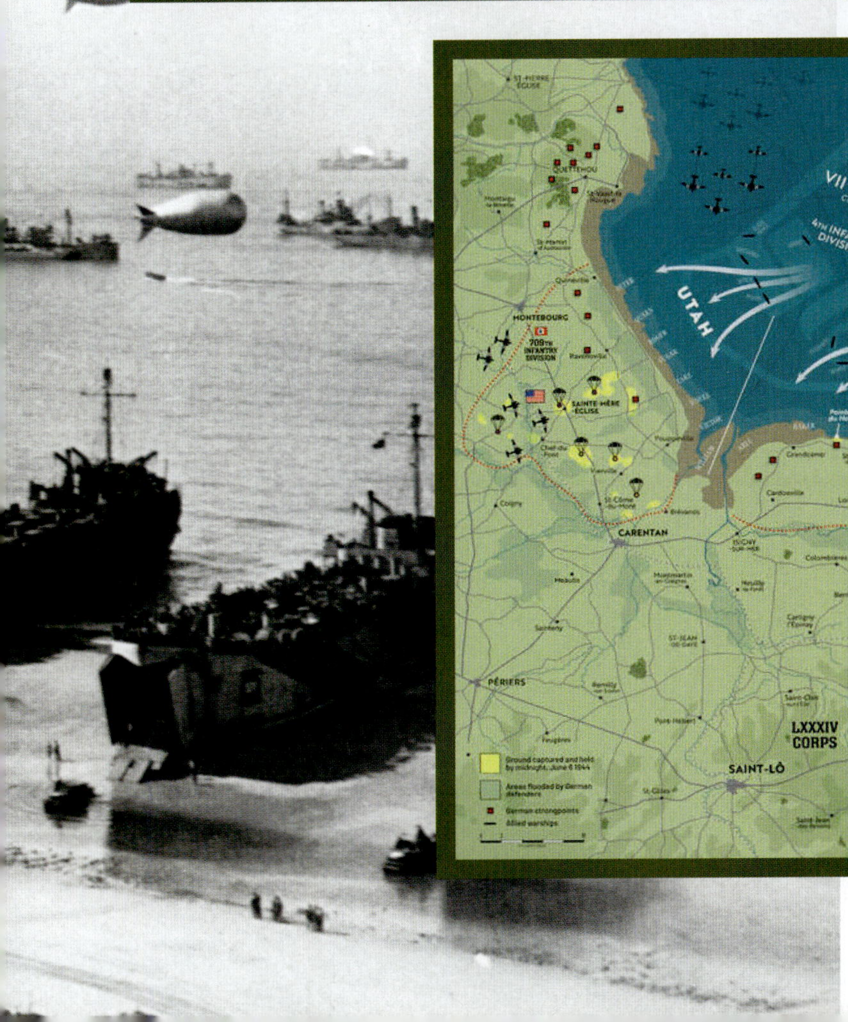

There were five landing zones along the Normandy coast where Allied forces launched the invasion of occupied France

KEY TECH

LCVP
'HIGGINS BOAT'

This simple but effectively designed vessel proved essential for Allied amphibious invasions across numerous operations

WORDS ANDREW WHITMARSH

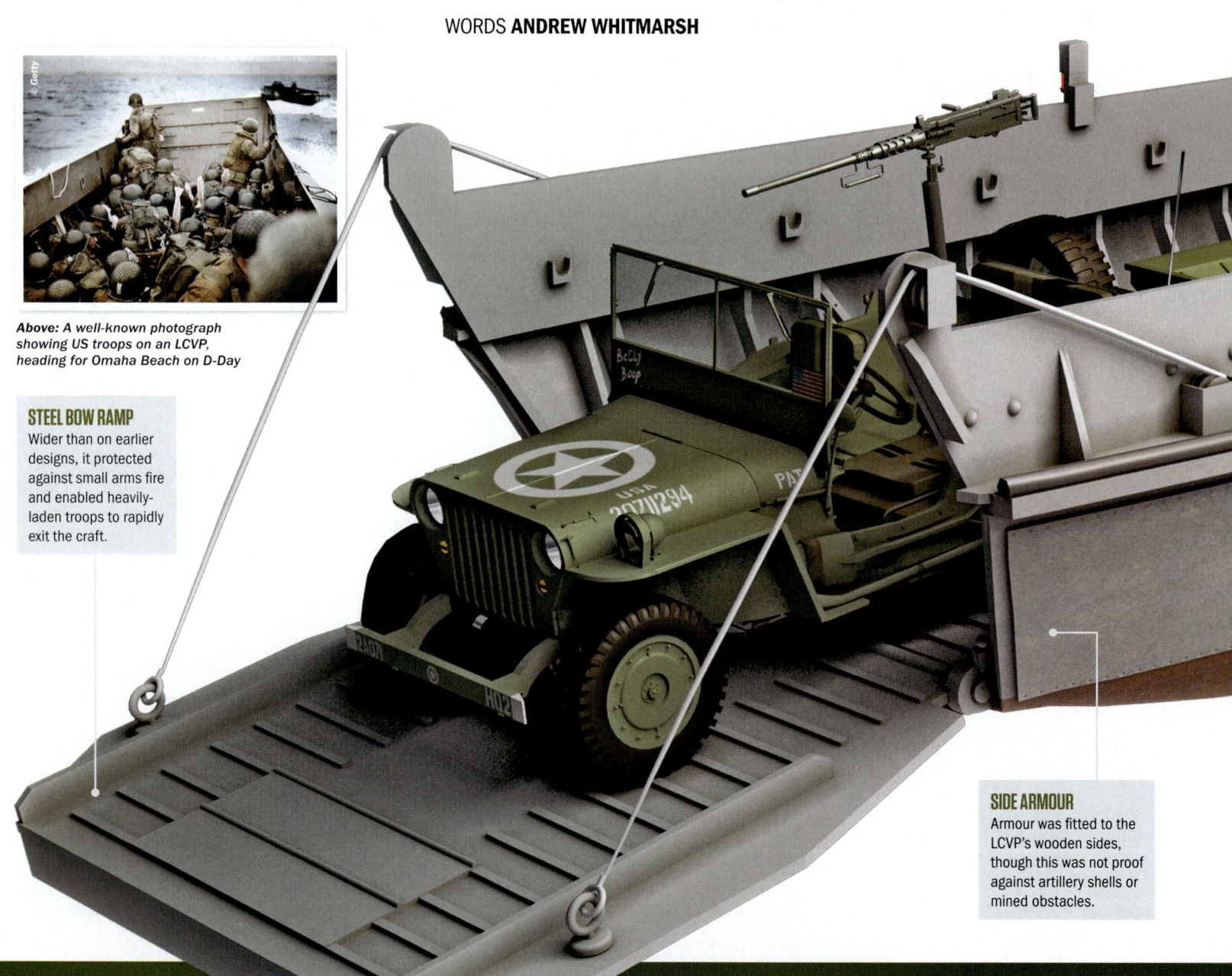

Above: A well-known photograph showing US troops on an LCVP, heading for Omaha Beach on D-Day

STEEL BOW RAMP
Wider than on earlier designs, it protected against small arms fire and enabled heavily-laden troops to rapidly exit the craft.

SIDE ARMOUR
Armour was fitted to the LCVP's wooden sides, though this was not proof against artillery shells or mined obstacles.

LCVP 'HIGGINS BOAT'

Landing craft had a crucial role in the Normandy Landings in 1944, but also in the Pacific theatre during the so-called 'Island-Hopping' campaign beginning in 1942. Although today they tend to be overlooked, that was certainly not the case at the time. Allied political and military leaders frequently debated how best to build or source sufficient landing craft for these vital operations.

An amphibious landing on an enemy-defended beach required specialist landing craft. These types were generally designed to be driven ashore, and then withdrawn after unloading troops or vehicles. Some types had other functions such as control or fire support.

The British naval official history states that Allied naval forces for the Normandy Landings comprised 6,939 vessels, including 4,126 landing ships and landing craft. This represents the total involved in Operation Neptune (6 to 30 June 1944), and some did not see operational service until after D-Day.

A proportion of those 4,126 vessels were in fact close relatives of landing craft, such as landing barges (mostly converted civilian river barges) or various types of the larger landing ships. All these types worked closely together: for example many smaller landing craft did not cross the English Channel under their own power but on board troop transport ships. Most types of landing craft used at Normandy were designed and built during the Second World War, mainly in the UK and the USA.

LANDING CRAFT, VEHICLE, PERSONNEL: LCVP

COMMISSIONED	FROM 1942
ORIGIN	USA
CAPACITY	36 TROOPS OR ONE LIGHT VEHICLE
LENGTH	36FT
RANGE	127 MILES, CARRIED ON A LARGER SHIP FOR LONG DISTANCES
ENGINE	HALL-SCOTT 250HP PETROL, OR GRAY 225HP DIESEL
CREW	3
ARMAMENTS	TWO .30-CAL. MACHINE GUNS (NOT ALWAYS FITTED)

POWERFUL ENGINE
The coxswain controlled the engine directly. The engine was used at low speed to hold the bow on the beach while unloading, and in reverse to unbeach.

MACHINE GUNS
In US use, LCVPs were sometimes fitted with a pair of .30-cal. machine guns to support the troops as they landed, but these were often omitted.

KEEL AND SKEG
The keel running under the craft was extended at the stern to form a skeg. This protected the rudder and propeller against damage when the LCVP beached to deliver its troops.

LANDING CRAFT, VEHICLE, PERSONNEL LCVP

Often referred to as a Higgins Boat after its designer, Higgins Industries of New Orleans, the LCVP was the standard American assault craft on D-Day. The three crew were a coxswain (steering), an engineer and a deck hand. Over 800 LCVPs were used at Normandy, about half of them in fact by British forces, not in the assault but for unloading follow-up troops. The British equivalent was the LCA (Landing Craft, Assault).

Both types had pros and cons but each nation tended to prefer the home-designed craft. The largest US transport ships (designated APA: Auxiliary Personnel, Attack) could carry 25-30 LCVPs, though that was only enough to land a proportion of the 1,200 or more troops on board. US-crewed LSTs (Landing Ship, Tank) each carried up to six LCVPs, and those from LSTs arriving earlier on D-Day were an important addition to the available assault craft.

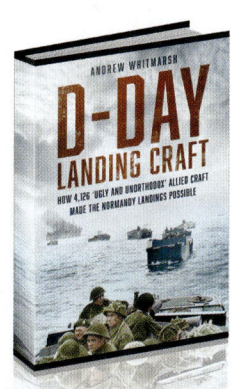

Andrew Whitmarsh is author of *D-Day Landing Craft* (published May 2024)

Illustration: Alex Pang

★ KEY BATTLE ★

SWORD BEACH

The easternmost sector of the 6 June Normandy Landings was a mostly British affair, and saw some of the biggest territorial gains of the first day of the Allied invasion

WORDS STEPHEN FISHER

British commandos of 1st Special Service Brigade landing on Queen Red sector of Sword Beach

SWORD BEACH

On 6 June 1944, the long-anticipated assault on occupied France took place along a 50 mile (80km) front – however the amphibious landings were confined to roughly 12 miles (19km) of beaches across five areas. One of the smallest landing areas was the easternmost, where the British 3rd Infantry Division would land on Queen White and Red beaches alongside the sleepy seaside town of Ouistreham.

Sword would be a tough nut to crack. The beach itself was well defended by the formidable stützpunkt 20, codenamed strongpoint Cod by the British, a significant company-sized fortification and the largest single strongpoint on all five of the Allies' landing zones.

To the east widerstandsnest 18 (Skate) was equipped with a 3in (75mm) anti-tank gun that could fire down the length of the beach, while widerstandsnest 21 (Trout) a little to the west could bring fire down on the attackers' right flank. A little recognised fact is that, although considerably narrower than Omaha Beach, the average strength of the defences per mile was practically the same on Sword.

Unlike Omaha, Sword was relatively low-lying and the attackers would not have to contend with the high bluffs that characterised the US beach. But unlike Omaha, 3 Division would have to deal with significant defences inland as well. Once off the beach, several artillery strongpoints and command posts barred the way, the strongest of which was widerstandsnest 17 (Hillman). Set into the broad Periers ridge 2 miles (3km) inland, it boasted numerous underground bunkers, steel cupolas and anti-tank guns. Moreover, its strength had been badly underestimated by Allied intelligence.

The British plan was a three-part assault. The first wave, led by 8 Infantry Brigade, would secure the beaches and the first towns inland. Behind them, 185 Brigade would come ashore and push rapidly south in the direction of Caen, hoping to secure the city by nightfall. 9 Brigade, the reserve formation, would push southwest to cover the right flank and link up with Canadian troops moving inland from Juno.

The invasion begins

At 2:50am, the first minesweepers arrived at the Lowering Position 9 miles (14.5km) off Queen Beach. For the next few hours, the sailing groups began to arrive and arrange themselves for the assault. At 5am the troopships were entering the designated area and preparing to lower their boats, while overhead dozens of aircraft droned past on their way to bomb Ouistreham.

On the left flank the battleships and cruisers of Force D took their places to begin bombarding the larger coastal batteries, but beyond them to the east a new threat emerged from the smoke screen laid by overhead aircraft. Three destroyer-sized torpedo boats of Korvetten-kapitän Henrich Hoffman's 5th Torpedo Boat Flotilla emerged from the swirling mists and immediately the big warship guns were brought to bear on the German warships. At 5:15am HMS Ramillies opened fire and for the next ten minutes great geysers of water erupted around the torpedo boats. Then, as soon as they had closed the range enough, Hoffman turned his boats beam on and let loose a volley of 16 torpedoes. As the enemy scurried back into the smoke, the ships of Force S took avoiding action. But for the Norwegian destroyer HNoMS Svenner there was no time – a torpedo slammed into her amidships and within minutes her back was broken.

There was no time for the fleet to mourn Svenner's loss – already the landing craft were setting course for Queen Beach. At the forefront on board LCH 185, Commander Edmund Currey studied the sea state. On his shoulders rested the responsibility of launching the swimming DD Sherman tanks that would lead the first waves of landing craft to the shore. As he lead the invasion force south he was relieved to see that while not perfect, the conditions were not so bad and, as they got nearer, he decided to go about a mile (1.6km) closer to the shore before launching the tanks from their landing craft.

At 6:30am the leading landing craft launched 34 DD tanks into the sea. Two quickly succumbed to the waves but the rest of these unlikely vessels struck out for the shore. Behind them the landing craft carrying the assault infantry and the Hobart's Funnies Armoured Vehicle Royal Engineers (AVRE) closed up.

A few minutes later, the bombardment started. A dozen destroyers opened fire on eight miles (13km) of shoreline, their 4.7in (120mm) shells hitting bunkers, strongpoints, trenches and reinforced houses. Behind the leading landing craft the guns of three artillery regiments opened up, firing their self-propelled 4in (105mm) guns from the decks of their landing craft. As they neared the shore the support landing craft joined the fray, including the fearsome Landing Craft Rockets, sending thousands of screeching rockets towards

Troops and a DD Sherman advance towards Ouistreham on 6 June

Medics attended to the wounded next to a Churchill tank

OPPOSING FORCES

GERMAN LAND FORCES VS ALLIED LAND FORCES

716 INFANTRY DIVISION AND 21 PANZER DIVISION

INFANTRY
The equivalent of five combat infantry battalions (within the Sword area)

ARMOUR
Approx. 100 armoured vehicles

ARTILLERY
Four coastal batteries fielding approximately 16 coastal artillery guns, 15 beach defence anti-tank guns and approximately 50 self-propelled and towed artillery pieces within the Sword area

GERMAN NAVAL FORCES
5th Torpedo Boat Flotilla (3 destroyer-sized torpedo boats), 15 Vorpostenboot Flotilla (6 escort whalers) and 4 & 10 Ramuboot Flotillas (11 minelayers)

BRITISH 3RD INFANTRY DIVISION, 27TH ARMOURED BRIGADE, 1ST SPECIAL SERVICE BRIGADE, 101 BEACH GROUP

INFANTRY
The equivalent of 13 combat infantry battalions (3rd Division troops plus commandos)

TANKS
Approx. 360 tanks (Shermans), Armoured Vehicle Royal Engineers (AVREs) and self-propelled anti-tank guns (M10s)

ARTILLERY
Three field regiments of self-propelled guns (Priests) totalling 72 guns

Allied Naval Forces: Force S

LANDING SHIPS
32 Landing Ship Infantry, Landing Ship Tank and Landing Ship HQ

MAJOR LANDING CRAFT
Approx. 200 Landing Craft Tank and Landing Craft Infantry (Large)

MINOR LANDING CRAFT
Approx. 110 Landing Craft Assault and Landing Craft Infantry (Small)

SUPPORT CRAFT
Approx. 60

BOMBARDMENT SHIPS
21 battleships, cruisers and destroyers

ESCORT SHIPS
66 minesweepers and corvettes

the beach. Above them hundreds of US B-17 bombers roared overhead, dropping thousands of tons of bombs on strongpoints along the shore and inland. Finally, when the leading craft were only half a mile (1km) from the shore, a squadron of Royal Canadian Air Force Typhoons roared down and dropped their bombs onto strongpoint Cod.

Almost as quickly as it began, the bombardment ceased, just as the leading tanks and landing craft approached the shore. But as soon as it did, the German defenders who had sheltered in their bunkers emerged and manned their guns. Shot and shell greeted the attackers as they ground up on the sand.

The effect was immediate. As it came ashore, the landing craft flotilla leader was hit by several shells and the commander of the AVRE assault squadrons was killed. While the tanks trapped behind his burning vehicle on the landing craft ramp fought to dislodge it the other AVRE troops came ashore, several succumbing to anti-tank fire.

Around them the DD tanks landed and sat in the shallows, pouring fire into houses and strongpoints as the waves lapped around their tracks. On the right flank the 1st South Lancashire Battalion raced across the sand and began breaching the barbed wire obstacles blocking the beach exits, but on the left the 2nd East Yorkshire Battalion faced the strong defences of Cod and Skate. Casualties mounted as withering fire was directed on the assault troops and very few complete units reached the top of the beach where they could start to clear the barbed wire.

As the assault troops battled for the beach, the follow-up units started to land. On the far left flank, 4 Commando came ashore in front of Skate and were instantly in action against the strongpoint. Along the length of the beach landing craft brought another squadron of tanks, but only one beach exit had so far been cleared. As the tide raced in, pushed by the stormy winds in the Channel, the beach narrowed and traffic jams grew as tanks, artillery, armoured cars and trucks sought to find dry sand and shelter from the shelling and mortar fire raining down on the beach. Meanwhile the assault troops were pushing through the defences and slowly surrounding

> "AS THE TIDE RACED IN, PUSHED BY THE STORMY WINDS IN THE CHANNEL, THE BEACH NARROWED AND TRAFFIC JAMS GREW"

and overwhelming the opposition. Spared the attention of the anti-tank guns the AVRE began to clear more exits, but it was slow work.

Having cleared the beach, at 8:20am 4 Commando began their advance on Ouistreham. Led by two troops of Free French commandos, the men jogged down the exposed mile-long (1.6km) straight road into the town, coming under increasingly heavy mortar and sniper fire as they did so. The two French troops peeled off and Commandant Kieffer took 1 Troop to neutralise the site of the town's old casino, since demolished and turned into a blockhouse.

Meanwhile 4 Commando advanced to the east end of the town and turned to attack the coastal artillery position at stützpunkt 8. Although it had already been bombed and fired on by HMS Frobisher, it was essential to make sure the battery's 6in (155mm) guns were neutralised. After rushing the outer defences the commando troops spread out to attack the gun positions, but were astounded to find them empty. After numerous air attacks the preceding week, the Germans had already withdrawn the guns inland.

On the right flank, 41 (RM) Commando pushed into Lion-sur-Mer, their objective to secure the town and link up with 47 (RM) Commando advancing from Juno Beach. As the commandos advanced they ran into strongpoint Trout, whose well-sited positions quickly rebuffed them. Three AVREs were summoned, but as they advanced along the main road towards the strongpoint they were picked off by an anti-tank gun. Then a strong German counter-attack pushed back 41 Commando's forward units and the Royal Marines were forced to fall back to the eastern edge of the town, only half a mile (0.8km) from the edge of the landing area. The invading forces wouldn't progress further west on D-Day.

While the commandos secured the flanks, 8 Infantry Brigade pushed south, and while the South Lancashires secured the town of Hermanville, the East Yorks advanced up to two strongpoints. Dozens of German soldiers had fallen back to stützpunkt 14, codenamed Sole, where they desperately tried to hold out against the British attacks.

Eventually forced back into the command bunker, their fanatical commander tried to hold out for as long as he could, until the Yorkshiremen brought up a flamethrower. In between them, 1 Special Service Brigade began its advance towards the bridges over the Caen Canal and Orne River, from where they would advance onto the heights overlooking Merville and Franceville-Plage.

Pushing ahead of the infantry, the commandos cut a path through Germans between Colleville and Benouville as they raced towards the bridges, which were thinly held by the airborne forces that had captured them. After midday the leading commandos reached the bridges and advanced.

Meanwhile, 1st Suffolk Battalion pushed into Colleville, securing another German battery that threatened the beaches. But as they advanced on strongpoint Hillman, their progress faltered. The German regimental HQ was much stronger than they had expected, and machine gun positions in armoured cupolas thwarted the first attack. With the position dominating the ridge on which it sat, only one battalion of infantry – the 1st King's Shropshire Light Infantry (KSLI) from 185 Brigade – was able to push past unmolested, while their fellow battalions in the brigade were forced to wait for Hillman to be neutralised. Supported by tanks of the Staffordshire Yeomanry, the KSLI advanced into the villages of Beuville and Bieville, but what was meant to be a brigade-sized thrust on Caen was now a slim and badly understrength push inland.

Meanwhile, the reserve brigade of infantry was coming ashore, but 9 Brigade's arrival was complicated by the traffic jams caused by

An M10 Wolverine self-propelled gun of 20th Anti-Tank Regiment

Erwin Rommel during an inspection of the defences in northern France, 1944

Obstacles, dubbed Rommel's Asparagus, were designed to hinder approaching landing craft

Troops and vehicles from the 185th Brigade Group, 3rd Infantry Division, British Second Army

the narrow beach and the congestion that had built up. With the entire right flank at risk of crumbling, two of the battalions were deployed to shore up the line facing west, while the third was despatched to strengthen the centre. 1 Suffolks made a second attack on Hillman while 2 East Yorks launched their attack on the final battery firing on the beaches, but it was not until the evening that both fell.

The two battalions of 185 Brigade tried to outflank Hillman, but the 1st Norfolk Battalion took heavy casualties and the 2nd Warwickshire Battalion went so far east that they were unable to reach 1 KSLI to support their advance.

Shortly after 4pm a new threat emerged, as nearly 100 armoured vehicles from 21 Panzer Division counter-attacked out of Caen. Although thinly stretched, the anti-tank guns of 1 KSLI and their supporting Shermans from the Staffordshire Yeomanry were well placed to repulse two of the columns advancing north and the Germans beat a hasty retreat to dig in on the Lebisey ridge between the British and Caen. A third column exploited the gap left open between Sword and Juno and raced to Lion-sur-Mer. But deprived of the tanks in the other two columns there was little they could do, and fearing the gap would close behind them they withdrew south that evening.

With the counter-attack blunted, 1 KSLI bravely attempted to secure the Lebisey ridge themselves, but the single battalion was unable to make any headway. As darkness fell they withdrew to positions around Bieville.

Aftermath

The following morning, supported by 1 Warwicks who were finally able to reach them, 1 KSLI put in a second attack on Lebisey, but this was similarly blunted and the British were forced to occupy a defensive line to the north.

Once the defenders of Lion-sur-Mer had pulled back, the British were able to fill the gap to their west and link up with the Canadian forces from Juno. But with their advance so badly hampered the previous day, and with fresh German reserves already arriving in the invasion area, a new front line was established north of Caen. It would be a month before the Allies could advance into the city.

Sword Beach had been a difficult battle. The well-defended landing area had caused in the region of 600 casualties on the beach alone, and the small landing area caused congestion for the following waves, who were not able to deploy inland quickly. The German counter-attack – the only armoured counter-attack anywhere in Normandy on D-Day – stalled the advance, but well-deployed British units were able to repulse it before it could reach the beaches, where the tanks would surely have caused chaos and carnage. Despite not taking Caen on D-Day, 3rd Infantry Division had managed to secure a strong presence on the eastern flank of the invasion area, link up with the airborne east of the river and protect the beaches from enemy armour. It was a victory and a key part in the success of 6 June.

> "WITH FRESH GERMAN RESERVES ALREADY ARRIVING IN THE INVASION AREA, A NEW FRONT LINE WAS ESTABLISHED NORTH OF CAEN. IT WOULD BE A MONTH BEFORE THE ALLIES COULD ADVANCE INTO THE CITY"

SWORD BEACH: THE UNTOLD STORY OF D-DAY'S FORGOTTEN VICTORY

Stephen Fisher's book *Sword Beach* tells the whole story of the easternmost amphibious landing area on D-Day.

KEY EVENT

THE RED BALL EXPRESS

Hastily arranged after the breakout famous convoy system that supplied overstretched Allied forces and was referred to by George S. Patton as "our most important weapon"

The GMC CCKW 'Jimmy' truck had a five-tonne cargo capacity and could be easily repaired, although it often suffered from burst tyres and had an average working life of less than a year

THE RED BALL EXPRESS

Before D-Day, the Allies were acutely aware that victory in Western Europe would depend on a permanent supply of fuel, ammunition, food and other materials for the front lines. The bombing of the French railway network handicapped the Germans but it also meant that the Allies were largely dependent on transportation by road.

During the Normandy Campaign, the Allies were able to build up supplies but after the breakout there was a huge advance across France. George S. Patton in particular aggressively sped across the country into Belgium, but the US Army soon began to run out of fuel. Large quantities of petrol were now far from the front and Patton emphasised its importance, "My men can eat their belts but my tanks gotta have gas!"

Men and trucks were brought together from different units to run on specially designated roads to quickly move the supplies. These routes were marked by red ball signs, which gave the convoy its nickname 'The Red Ball Express'. From 21 August 1944, approximately 12,500 tonnes of supplies were carried each day to the constantly changing frontlines.

At its peak, the Express operated almost 6,000 vehicles (mostly GMC CCKW 'Jimmy' trucks) and three quarters of its personnel were African American soldiers. Although they suffered from discrimination, these men would overload their trucks and exceed the official speed limit to get supplies through, despite frequently coming under fire.

The route from Cherbourg to Chartres, south-west of Paris, took teams of two or three around 27 hours without stopping. By the time the Express ended on 16 November 1944, when the port facilities at Antwerp became open, drivers completed an average round-trip that could be as long as 600 miles. Nevertheless the convoy had done its job with Eisenhower calling it the "lifeline between combat and supply".

US veteran Pete Shaw was among those who participated in the Express, with the 283rd Field Artillery Battalion. "It was awesome. They used all the trucks they could to go back into France to get supplies because there was no gas for the tanks or ammunition," he recalled. "It was 24 hours a day and each truck had three drivers and four ammunition handlers to go into all these places."

Corporal Charles Johnson of 783rd Military Police Battalion waves on a convoy near Alençon, France, 5 September 1944

It is estimated that the Red Ball Express transported over 400,000 tonnes of materials to the Allied front lines

KEY TECH

SHERMAN FIREFLY

British ingenuity brought the Sherman tank's main weapon to reasonable parity with the German Panther and Tiger during WWII

WORDS **MIKE HASKEW**

The Sherman tank was nimble and reliable in the field, and most of all it was available in great numbers from late 1942 through to the end of World War II. Approximately 50,000 of the American-built tanks were manufactured from 1941-45, and the Sherman became the primary armoured fighting vehicle of Allied armies around the world.

When the Sherman debuted with the British Eighth Army at the Battle of El Alamein in North Africa, October 1942, its 75mm gun was capable of dealing with the German PzKpfw. III and PzKpfw. IV tanks deployed with Panzer Armee Afrika. However, as German factories began turning out more powerful tanks, particularly the PzKpfw. V Panther and PzKpfw. VI Tiger, mounting high velocity 75mm and 88mm cannon respectively, the Sherman was at a decided disadvantage.

The tank's original main armament, the short barrelled M2 and its derivative M3 with a longer barrel (both 75mm guns) rapidly became inadequate in armoured combat. The 75's low muzzle velocity along with the increased armour protection of the latest German tanks rendered the gun ineffective at appreciable distance, while the German tanks were often able to destroy a Sherman prior to the Allied tank manoeuvring into reasonable firing range.

Although the Sherman had been conceived as a breakthrough weapon, tank versus tank combat in the hedgerows of France and beyond was inevitable. The Americans sought a solution to the firepower disadvantage with the high-velocity 76mm M1 gun. British tankers and engineers settled on their own high-velocity weapon, a modified version of the Ordnance QF 17-pounder anti-tank gun. The resulting variant was nicknamed the Firefly due to its substantial muzzle flash. The resulting combination of speed and firepower redefined the capabilities of the Sherman tank from D-Day to the end of the war.

> **"THE RESULTING SHERMAN VARIANT WAS NICKNAMED THE FIREFLY DUE TO ITS SUBSTANTIAL MUZZLE FLASH WHEN THE 17-POUNDER DISCHARGED"**

Continental manufactured the R975 aircraft engine for use in armoured vehicles. During World War II the company produced more than 53,000 R975s

ENGINE
Three Sherman tank models were converted in British facilities to the Firefly configuration. The M4 and M4 composite, named due to both cast and welded hull components, were powered by the Continental R975 9-cylinder radial gasoline engine capable of generating up to 400 horsepower, while the M4A4 variant utilised the 470-horsepower Chrysler A57 multibank gasoline engine. The Continental R975 was originally an aircraft engine, modified for use in armoured vehicles, and the hull of the Sherman was lengthened slightly to accommodate the rear-mounted, 30-cylinder Chrysler A57. The top speed for the Sherman Firefly reached 40 kilometres (25 miles) per hour.

SHERMAN FIREFLY

A Sherman Firefly patrols the Meuse at Namur during the Battle of the Bulge

SHERMAN FIREFLY

COMMISSIONED:	1943
CREW:	4
ORIGIN:	USA / BRITAIN
LENGTH:	7.77 METERS (25 FEET, 6 INCHES) OVERALL
RANGE:	193 KILOMETRES (120 MILES)
ENGINE:	CONTINENTAL R975 C-1 9-CYLINDER RADIAL GASOLINE ENGINE
PRIMARY WEAPON:	1 X QF 17-POUNDER ANTI-TANK GUN
SECONDARY WEAPON:	1 X COAXIALLY MOUNTED 7.62MM (.30-CAL.) BROWNING M1919 MACHINE GUN; 1 X TOP MOUNTED 12.7MM (.50 CAL.) BROWNING M2 MACHINE GUN

INTERIOR

The standard five-man crew of the Sherman tank was reduced to four with the Firefly. The hull gunner, or co-driver, position was vacated in order to provide space for the large projectiles fired by the 17-pounder gun. The confines of the turret presented challenges for the accommodation of the big weapon as well. The Firefly commander was positioned to the rear of the turret with the loader forward and left of the gun breech, and the gunner forward to the right. The driver was seated in the front of the hull to the left and operated the gearbox with levers.

> "THE HULL GUNNER, OR CO-DRIVER, POSITION WAS VACATED IN ORDER TO PROVIDE SPACE FOR THE LARGE PROJECTILES FIRED BY THE 17-POUNDER GUN"

The driver position in the Sherman tank chassis is situated forward in the hull and to the left. The tillers the driver used to operate the tank are visible in front

Above: *The cramped interior of the conventional Sherman tank was made even tighter with the addition of the Firefly's heavy 17-pounder*

DESIGN

Several design modifications were required to convert the Sherman tank to the more-powerful Firefly. The weapon itself was reconfigured with recoil cylinders shortened and relocated to the sides, while the breech was rotated 90 degrees for side loading and the gun cradle shortened to accommodate the 17-pounder. The tank's radio was moved to a steel box called a bustle, which was welded to the rear of the turret. Since the gun consumed a considerable amount of space, a second hatch was built into the top of the turret to allow the crew to bail out if the tank caught fire during battle.

SHERMAN FIREFLY

Left: A Firefly crew of 1st Northamptonshire Yeomanry load ammunition for the 17-pounder prior to Operation Totalise

While German tanks were prone to mechanical failure, the Sherman was robust and easily serviced in the field

The 17-pounder gun of the Sherman Firefly extended considerably longer than the original 75mm weapon mounted with the tank

ARMAMENT

The Ordnance QF 17-pounder anti-tank gun was a high-velocity 76.2mm (3-inch) weapon designed to replace the 6-pounder gun that was rapidly becoming obsolete during World War II. Development began in 1940, and a production line was established the following spring. As German PzKpfw. VI Tiger tanks reached North Africa in 1943, the 17-pounder was rushed into service. Full production began that year, and its armour-piercing ammunition proved capable of defeating the latest German tanks. Major George Brighty and Lieutenant Colonel George Witheridge are credited with the idea of pairing the Sherman tank with the 17-pounder to produce the Firefly.

85

LIBERATION OF PARIS

25 August 1944

After days of fighting between the Resistance and the Germans, Paris is finally liberated by the Allies, led by the French 2nd Armoured Division and the US 4th Infantry Division. The city had been under Nazi occupation for four years, and the following day a celebratory liberation parade was held on the Champs-Élysées.

LIBERATION OF PARIS

87

KEY BATTLE

LIBERATION OF THE PHILIPPINES

One of the more difficult island campaigns in WWII's Pacific Theatre saw a brutal months-long fight that exhausted Japan's military strength

WORDS **MIGUEL MIRANDA**

LIBERATION OF THE PHILIPPINES

After the last American garrison surrendered in April 1942 the Philippines endured 40 months of Japanese occupation. Ending it was a matter of honour for General Douglas MacArthur and his staff, all of them exiled after defeat in the Philippines. In the summer of 1944 they were raring to go after achieving victory in the South Pacific and the crucial New Guinea archipelago.

As commander of Allied forces in the Southwest Pacific there was little need for MacArthur to spend weeks building up the invasion force. The plans were already detailed and involved a gradual conquest of the Philippine archipelago.

Red Beach

The importance of the Philippines to Japan's maritime routes justified a build-up that reached more than 400,000 troops in 1944. Overall command was the responsibility of General Terauchi Hisaichi and by September the celebrated veteran General Tomoyuki Yamashita was put in charge of the grouping known as the 35th Army.

Considering the resources at their disposal the headquarters in Manila were bewildered by the growing evidence of an American invasion from the east. When the small island of Morotai, some 373 miles (600km) from Mindanao, was quickly seized there was no rush to organise a counter-offensive by sea. In the beginning of October there were signs of US naval activity getting nearer and nearer to the Visayas, but Japanese HQ in Manila could not prepare a credible defense fast enough.

Yamashita's role was not without controversy. Though immortalised by his triumph over the Allies in Malaya and Singapore, as well as finishing the conquest of Luzon, his career was scuttled by a sudden assignment to Manchuria, which was far removed from any serious combat. Hailed a national hero by the press and respected in the Japanese government, Yamashita arrived in the Philippines as a subordinate tasked with achieving impossible results.

On 17 October a large US Navy commando raid on the island of Samar secured an outpost on Guiuan, and the small island could now be used for observing any traffic entering or leaving the Leyte Gulf. This was the work of the 6th Ranger Battalion under Colonel Henry Mucci. The mustachioed leader of the unit organised the preparation of his men in New Guinea with laborious marches across challenging terrain and small-unit training. The Rangers were in excellent physical shape and equipped for surprise attacks on poorly defended Japanese installations like the ones on Samar island that blocked the way to Leyte island.

On the day after the preemptive raids on Samar the navy's minesweepers arrived in Leyte Gulf. A stream of alarming reports from the Visayas alerted the Japanese headquarters in Manila that six aircraft carriers and ten battleships were steaming toward the Leyte-Samar cluster trailed by more than 100 transports. To Hisaichi's dismay the contingency known as Sho Operation No 1 was making slow progress and naval reinforcements from Formosa and Singapore would take days until they arrived in the Visayas.

Come daybreak on 20 October the shoreline of Palo, a district in Leyte facing San Pablo Bay, was shaken by the preparatory US bombardment meant to scatter the outnumbered Japanese defenders stationed there. At least a full division was dispersed along the eastern shoreline of Leyte without sufficient tanks or large-calibre artillery. Thanks to the communications and signals intelligence provided by local Filipino guerrillas, the transports carrying the US Sixth Army made it to shore in dramatic fashion.

On the first day of Operation King II, the name chosen for the Leyte campaign, elements from four infantry divisions disembarked amid heavy gunfire. Vital to this successful insertion were the Landing Ship, Tank (LST) transports that drove all the way to the unobstructed beaches and quickly discharged men and vehicles from their ramps. Despite the constant gunfire from the hidden Japanese riflemen scattered along the defensive line on the strip of land called Red Beach, a single transport parked on a sand bar to discharge MacArthur and members of his staff. Surrounded by his trusted veterans who'd been with him since the doomed effort to hold back the Japanese in 1942, a brief press conference was held before the general departed.

Two days later the city of Tacloban was recaptured after an inadequate defence by demoralised Japanese, who abandoned their half-finished tunnels. While establishing MacArthur's temporary headquarters in the palatial home of an American businessman, accommodation was also made for the VIP in his entourage: Sergio Osmeña. The former vice president of the Philippine Commonwealth was now slated to assume the role of interim president once American troops reached Luzon and Manila was retaken.

Constant rain, endless mud

While LSTs and other transports continued delivering supplies to Red Beach the naval Battle of Leyte Gulf unfolded from 23-25 October, during which the Imperial Japanese Navy (IJN) tried to wipe out the vulnerable American light carriers and their destroyer escorts. Admiral William Halsey and Admiral Thomas Kincaid's task forces prevailed with considerable losses of planes,

American howitzers laying down fire in Leyte. Japanese ground forces had nothing to match these weapons' range or destructive power

but the IJN suffered even greater casualties, including the loss of hundreds of its carrier-based fighters. IJN reinforcements steaming from the Borneo coast were also decimated as they tried crossing the Sibuyan Sea to reach Leyte Gulf on 24 October. They were met by a relentless hail of bombs and torpedoes from American carrier-based fighters, resulting in the loss of the Musashi and four other battleships.

These reversals saved the thousands of American troops that had arrived in Leyte and Samar, forcing the Japanese headquarters in Manila to continue the fight with whatever resources it could scramble. Growing desperation led to waves of futile air strikes on Sixth Army positions, including the airstrip being laid down outside Tacloban for the Fifth Air Force's bombers, and tokko tai ('special attack') assaults where the Japanese pilots crashed their planes into American ships. These efforts were ineffective but it was not until the following year when these suicidal tactics earned their moniker: kamikaze.

Because of the island's difficult geography there was no single battle that won Leyte for the Americans. Combat was a slog that went on day and night, week after week. As well as the persistent Japanese aerial attacks from Luzon, another hindrance was the foul weather. Seasonal rains turned the ground into sodden mush and, like most provinces of the Philippines, the inadequate roads outside the towns and cities bogged down any motor transport in thick mud. For weeks on end torrential rain tormented the American troops – young men who had never been in a tropical climate before. The sergeants and corporals who were veterans of Guadalcanal and New Guinea fared better, and unlike those difficult campaigns in the Southwest Pacific the men were provided with freshly packaged rations. From the perspective of wartime logistics it was an absolute marvel that by 1944 it was possible for American troops in Asia to enjoy air-dropped ice cream. Crucially, the ever-present scourge of tropical disease was mitigated by improved battlefield evacuation and access to doctors.

US air superiority was close at hand by month's end, but thousands of Japanese troops were still arriving by ship in Ormoc, the city about 30 miles (50km) west of Tacloban. Neither side could launch a single offensive to secure their beachheads as Leyte's interior mountains and ridges blocked any movement. This made the constant presence of localised air power crucial. Once the Fifth Air Force's P-38 interceptors began arriving in late October the heavy twin-tailed aircraft flew endless sorties to fend off Japanese incursions. American fighters were also busy eliminating Japanese merchant ships and naval transports attempting to reach Ormoc. The month-and-a-half spent securing the whole island, a task that dragged on with less intensity into 1945, saw Japanese forces in the island reached anywhere from 80,000 to 100,000.

Among the multitude of combatants who vied for the island a rare standout was the peerless Major Richard 'Dick' Bong, whose aerial kills reached such proportions in a single month that the Fifth Air Force's commander General George Kenney arranged for his spectacular send off. Having confirmed a 40th kill and a record of 500 flying hours, a ceremony was held in Tacloban for Bong to personally receive a Medal of Honor from MacArthur. It was inspiring copy for the journalists in attendance. As an additional reward, Kenney arranged for the major's return home to the United States, where a new career as a test pilot awaited. Examining the facts of the Major's achievements is remarkable: from 1943 until December 1944 this 'Ace of Aces' collected a Medal of Honor, a Distinguished Service Cross, two Silver Stars, seven Flying Crosses and 13 Air Medals. As a matter of perspective, Japan's aerial losses in the Visayas in late 1944 reached around 1,000 planes, with several hundred shot down in and around Leyte.

From Leyte To Luzon

With at least two corps-sized US formations ensconced in Leyte by December and local air superiority achieved, the Japanese army's headquarters in Manila faced a daunting task. The Philippines had to be defended at any cost to prevent American invasions of the island chain leading to Japan itself. In fact, until 1943 the Department of War's strategy for the Pacific was to seize Formosa and establish a maritime logistical corridor that reached the Chinese coast. Of course, this plan was altered after the clash in the Philippine Sea in June the following year and the Philippines, where former American bases were occupied by Japan, was considered better suited for supporting the new long-range bombers that could be deployed in the theatre.

Yamashita was now in charge of all operations in the Philippines and his bid to hold Leyte was a costly failure. It was obvious to him the Americans would beat a path to Luzon and reach Manila. A last ditch offensive was carried out on 6 December involving elite paratroopers dropped in eastern Leyte. Armed with thermite bombs they were tasked with blowing up American fuel depots in the airfields laid down during the

Over the course of a month the US Sixth Army's 200,000 men fought to capture Leyte from the Japanese

LIBERATION OF THE PHILIPPINES

Local guerrillas provided the US forces with vital intelligence before and during the Leyte campaign

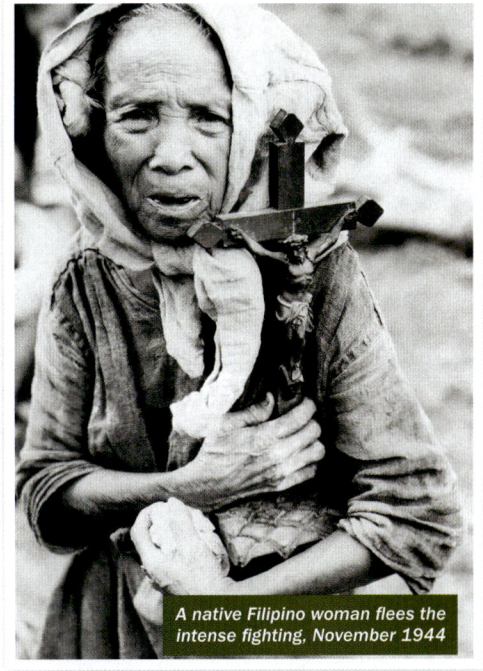
A native Filipino woman flees the intense fighting, November 1944

"THE IMPORTANCE OF THE PHILIPPINES TO JAPAN'S MARITIME ROUTES JUSTIFIED A BUILD-UP THAT REACHED MORE THAN 400,000 TROOPS IN 1944"

previous month. If this was achieved survivors were expected to hold off countless American troops until reinforcements arrived on foot. Not surprisingly this offensive was a failure too. The fighting dragged on for a week and dissipated as American forces reached Ormoc and cut off the island from any relief. As a calculated morale boost Leyte was declared secure on Christmas Day, but this did not mean the fighting in the island came to an end. At that point it remained difficult to ascertain how many Japanese stragglers had sought refuge in the impenetrable wilderness and perhaps nearby Samar.

Since its arrival in October the Sixth Army had the advantage of a sizable local resistance movement that enhanced its intelligence gathering. According to official US Army records of the campaign, the landings on 20 October were assisted by guerrillas whose numbers had grown to more than several thousand. Anti-Japanese resistance in the Philippines was not only fuelled by hatred for the occupier but a strong belief that the United States would eventually liberate the country; it was a sentiment that MacArthur never hesitated to promote. This belief was helped along by American survivors who had eluded capture and withdrawn to remote areas where they organised small company-sized groups.

The other varieties of guerrillas were Philippine Army veterans and minor officials who were being targeted by the Japanese. At least 40 different guerrilla formations emerged throughout the Philippines from 1942 to 1943. They were helped along by clandestine missions where submarines supplied weapons and portable radio sets. In return, the guerrillas filled their ranks and fed intelligence to the US Navy. In Leyte, once-disorganised guerrillas were consolidated under the command of Colonel Ruperto K Kangleon and their numbers exceeded 3,000 men and women.

Undaunted by a constant shortage of weapons, the guerrillas helped American troops as scouts and guides as the gruelling jungle warfare in Leyte's forested areas dragged on for weeks.

By the time newly built airstrips were operational on the island of Mindoro by December, the divisions that fought in Leyte were reorganised under a corps-sized formation and reached Luzon by 15 December. Rather than try and delay the Americans, a now desperate Yamashita sought to preserve the remainder of his forces and separated them, organising three groups that were tasked with holding certain areas in Luzon for an indefinite period. On 3 March 1945 the Japanese naval infantry's desperate holdouts in the capital Manila were finally flushed out by American troops after three hellish weeks of urban combat. It was the last significant battle in the Philippines.

Landing Ship, Tank transports discharge men and equipment onto the shoreline

KEY BATTLE

BAGRATION

After suffering the horror of Germany's 1941 invasion of the Motherland, the Red Army responded with a ferocious offensive

WORDS **WILL LAWRENCE**

With Hitler fighting on a second front in France, Stalin turned his attention to Belorussia and the last remaining undefeated German force on the Eastern Front, launching Operation Bagration on 22 June 1944. If successful, Bagration – named after a prince who fought during the Napoleonic Wars – would lay bare the German heartland in East Prussia and allow Soviet tanks to roll towards Königsberg. The road to Berlin would then be exposed. Stalin's chosen date was significant; it marked the third anniversary of Hitler's attack on the Motherland.

In the days leading up to the operation's commencement, partisan groups launched a series of attacks on the German rear, using more than 40,000 demolition charges as they sought to disrupt the railway lines that supplied Army Group Centre (one of the three army groupings organised by the Wehrmacht at the start of the Barbarossa campaign). A short artillery bombardment opened proceedings at 4am on 22 June before the major offensive developed on the following day.

The Soviet forces assembled for Bagration comprised 166 divisions, of which 124, including six cavalry divisions, featured in the initial assault. In addition, more than 6,000 aircraft organised into five air armies (one supporting each Front except the First Belorussian, where two were allocated), provided valuable support.

The attack began at 5am, with a massive aerial bombardment as the Soviet forces attempted to weaken the strongest German positions. The 3rd Panzer Army had secreted itself in marshy terrain surrounding the city of Vitebsk and now found itself subjected to an intense artillery and rocket bombardment. Units also attempted to create holes in the 3rd Army's salient line, launching a series of coordinated attacks.

On 23 June, with the Third Army weakened, the full weight of the Soviet offensive began. Hitler had designated Vitebsk a 'fortified city' (to be held to the last man), and by nightfall on the 24th, two German divisions were completely encircled. It would only be a matter of days before the Red Army was able to completely wipe out the German 3rd Army – some 28,000 men. Meanwhile, the 4th Army struggled to hold key positions on the Minsk-

Above German prisoners captured by troops of the Belorussian Fronts are marched through the streets of Moscow in July 1944

Moscow road under a constant onslaught of tanks fitted with mine-rollers and flamethrowers under the command of General Ivan Chernyakhovsky.

On 26 June that Field Marshal Ernst Busch flew to Germany to attempt to force the Führer to relent on the no-retreat policy, which had so far condemned large portions of his army to death. Enraged, Hitler instead replaced Busch, with Field Marshal Walther Model made head of the Führer's forces in the area. Nonetheless, by the evening of 26 June, German commanders decided to retreat to more defensible lines anyway, opening the road to the Red Army advance.

The day after Busch's arrival, the city of Borisov at the Berezina crossing point fell, resulting in 40,000 German troops becoming trapped east of Bobruisk. This too would fall on 29 June, and some 50,000 German soldiers were slaughtered in under a week by the 1st Belorussian Front alone. One week after Bagration's commencement, its first phase had shattered German resistance. The three German armies had lost 130,000 men killed and more than 60,000 as prisoners of war, along with 900 tanks destroyed or put out of action. This was a crippling blow to Army Group Centre and a vast gap was opening on Germany's Eastern Front.

On 2 July, Hitler conceded that Minsk was lost and thousands were killed or captured in the encirclement. With Minsk now under their control, the Soviet forces expanded their initial goals and were ordered to push towards the Lithuanian and Polish borders.

The Lithuanian capital was in Soviet hands by 10 July, and the Third Belorussian Front had finally set foot on German territory. A week later, Stalin was formally celebrating the success of Operation Bagration by parading German POWs through the streets of Moscow.

The crushing of Army Group Centre reverberated across the Eastern Front, from the Balkans to the Baltic, and left the Red Army poised to launch an attack across the Vistula, the largest river in Poland. When that watery barricade was crossed, the rest of East Prussia would be prone; for the first time, the Third Reich's very own soil was under threat.

Occurring at the same time as Operation Bagration, Soviet forces also launched the Lvov-Sandomierz Offensive. Here time the intention was to push further into Poland and Ukraine and capture the cities of Lublin and Lvov. On 13 July, Marshall Ivan Konev's 1st Ukrainian Front attacked the battered remains of Model's forces, beginning with a heavy artillery bombardment. Over successive days, the 3rd Soviet Army found itself initially unable to make much progress against the 4th Panzers commanded by Colonel Josef Harpe, but by 18 July they had pushed them back along the entire front.

By 20 July a wedge had been driven between the 1st Panzer and 4th Panzer armies, and by the 27th the 1st Panzer Army was forced to abandon Lvov, retreating into the Carpathians. Meanwhile, the 4th Panzer Army found itself pushed into southern Poland, where it would remain until January 1945. Using the shattered remains of his army, Model desperately attempted to stop the oncoming advance, but it was a lost cause. By August the Red Army had reached the outskirts of Warsaw and Model had been transferred to the Western Front. In just over a single month the German forces had lost some 350,000 men.

Soviet propaganda from the time urged the Red Army to 'beat the German beasts'

Soviet soldiers on the offensive near Leningrad

THE ADVANCE

THE DNIEPER OFFENSIVE
AUGUST - DECEMBER 1943

In the aftermath of the great victory at Kursk, the Red Army launched its drive to the Dnieper in August 1943. Stalin hurled his armies along a broad front totalling some 850 miles as he sought control of the pivotal industrial regions of the Donbas and the breadbasket of east Ukraine. The historian John Erickson numbers the Soviet armies engaged in this assault at more than 2.5 million soldiers, organised in five fronts, with 2,400 tanks and assault guns. The outnumbered Germans still had 1 million men to resist the onslaught, though they were eventually forced back across the Dnieper's western shore.

LENINGRAD–NOVGOROD OFFENSIVE
JANUARY - MARCH 1944

Launched by the Red Army in January 1944, the Leningrad-Novgorod Offensive opened with a strike against German Army Group North by the Soviet Volkov and Leningrad Fronts, along with part of the Second Baltic Front, all of which came under the command of General Popov. The aim was to lift the German Siege of Leningrad and position the Red Army for an offensive against the Baltic states. By 26 January, the city was free, the Soviets having cleared the Moscow-Leningrad railway. German bastions then toppled day by day as the Wehrmacht forces were pushed back to the River Narva.

DNIEPER–CARPATHIAN OFFENSIVE
DECEMBER 1943 - APRIL 1944

On Christmas Eve 1943, the Red Army initiated offensive operations designed to clear German forces from the rest of Ukraine and also to free the Crimea. A massed artillery barrage launched from an area south-east of Kiev announced the assault, as the Soviets sought to batter a route for General Vatutin's First Ukrainian Front. Dubbed by Stalin as the 'Liberation of the Right-Bank Ukraine', the movement incorporated the Red Army's First, Second, Third and Fourth Ukrainian Fronts, as well the First and Second Belorussian Fronts.

OPERATION BAGRATION
JUNE - AUGUST 1944

Stalin's huge push against Army Group Centre inflicted extremely heavy casualties on the Wehrmacht and ranks as one of Germany's heaviest reverses of World War II. After the destruction of Army Group Centre's Fourth Army, Third Panzer Army and Ninth Army, the Soviet forces reached the strategically important Vistula River, and Warsaw lay threatened. The havoc rained on Army Group Centre saw East Prussia exposed, with the inhabitants of the Reich for the first time lying at the mercy of the Red Army. A vast amount of Soviet territory was also liberated from German occupation.

BALTIC OFFENSIVE
SEPTEMBER - NOVEMBER 1944

On 14 September, the Soviets committed three Fronts to the destruction of Germany's Army Group North in the Baltic states. Almost 1 million Red Army soldiers were deployed along a 300-plus mile stretch, though they found it tough going. Army Group North contained many of Germany's most battle-hardened Eastern divisions, who regularly counterattacked across the fens and marshes. The Soviet push resulted in the isolation of 30 German divisions in the Courland pocket between Tukums and Libau. Despite furious fighting, elements of Army Group Courland held out until May 1945.

JASSY–KISHINEV, BUDAPEST AND BELGRADE OFFENSIVES
AUGUST - DECEMBER 1944

The Jassy-Kishinev operation saw the Red Army's Second and Third Ukrainian Fronts ordered to destroy Axis forces as they pushed through Romania ahead of the final offensives of that year, in the Carpathians and towards the key cities of Budapest, Bucharest and Belgrade. All of these movements formed the latter part of Stalin's 'Ten Blows', designed to crack German resistance along the Soviets Western Front. By the time the Blows were complete, the German heartland was exposed and the road to Berlin was open.

KEY OPERATIONS

A **KURSK:** 5 JULY – 23 AUGUST 1943
B **BELGOROD-KHARKOV OFFENSIVE:** 12-23 AUGUST 1943
C **BATTLE OF SMOLENSK:** 7 AUGUST – 2 OCTOBER 1943
D **BATTLE OF KIEV:** 3 NOVEMBER – 22 DECEMBER 1943
E **BATTLE OF NARVA:** 2 FEBRUARY – 10 AUGUST 1944
F **BATTLE OF TANNENBERG LINE:** 25 JULY – 10 AUGUST 1944
G **COURLAND POCKET POST BALTIC OFFENSIVE:** 14 SEPTEMBER – 24 NOVEMBER 1944
H **BATTLE OF DEBRECEN:** 6-29 OCTOBER 1944
I **BATTLE OF BELGRADE:** 28 SEPTEMBER – 20 OCTOBER 1944
J **BATTLE OF BUDAPEST:** 29 DECEMBER 1944 – 13 FEBRUARY 1945
K **WARSAW UPRISING (FAILED):** 1 AUGUST – 2 OCTOBER 1944

Churchill, Roosevelt and Stalin in the grounds of the Livadia Palace, Yalta

VICTORY
1945

The final steps in the path to victory over the Axis powers included some of the bloodiest fighting of the war. Major campaigns in Europe converged in the invasion of Germany from both east and west, culminating in the unconditional surrender of Nazi Germany. With war still raging in the Pacific and South-East Asian theatres, the Allies continued to push Japanese forces back towards the Home Islands and unleashed nuclear weapons to bring an end to the conflict.

★ 4 FEBRUARY 1945 ★

THE YALTA CONFERENCE

Initially hailed as a success, the leaders' meeting laid the foundations for the Cold War and had repercussions that remain with us today

WORDS **JOHN BEALES**

THE YALTA CONFERENCE

With the Allied victory in Europe seemingly inevitable, the 'Big Three' leaders Roosevelt, Churchill and Stalin met in the Crimean resort town of Yalta between 4-11 February 1945. The aims of the conference were to discuss the progress of the war and the securing of the unconditional surrender of Germany, to agree the future of Germany and Eastern Europe, and to discuss plans for the United Nations organisation: the UN being construed as the mechanism to manage and enforce the post-war world order.

Britain and the USA supported a Polish government-in-exile in London, while the Soviets supported a communist-dominated Polish Committee on National Liberation installed in Soviet-occupied eastern Poland. With an eye on the continuing war against Japan, and expected heavy casualties, the USA and Britain wanted to secure Soviet participation in the conflict in the Pacific region and secure free elections in Eastern Europe. But their desire to create a world based on collective security and the self-determination of the liberated territories of Europe would ultimately be dashed.

Stalin demanded that the Soviet Union be bordered by 'friendly' governments and that Eastern and Central Europe become a Soviet sphere of influence, and demanded that it keep the areas of eastern Poland it had annexed in 1939. Stalin also made Mongolia's independence of China a precondition for agreeing to join the war against Japan, alongside other conditions: the recognition of Manchuria as a Soviet sphere of influence; the return of South Sakhalin Island; the cession of the Kuril Islands from Japan; and a share in the operation of the Manchurian railroads. In return, Stalin agreed to enter the war with Japan within three months of the war in Europe ending.

The three leaders agreed that Germany was to be demilitarised and denazified, and war criminals pursued and prosecuted. Germany was also to pay reparations that included the supply of labour: the Soviet Union ultimately using millions of former German prisoners of war and deporting ethnic Germans from Poland and elsewhere as forced labour in industries ranging from agriculture to plutonium mining. Many would die, as would many of the Soviet citizens that had fallen into German hands and whom it was agreed would be forcibly returned to the Soviet Union.

General Charles de Gaulle, leader of the Free French forces, was not invited to the Yalta Conference but France was given one of the four zones of occupation in Germany, although it was to be formed from territories initially included in the American and British zones. Berlin was similarly divided into four zones.

The United Nations Charter of 1945 proposed a core permanent Security Council membership comprised of the United States, Great Britain, Russia, China and France: Stalin agreed to join because the voting formula enabled permanent Security Council members to veto decisions deemed not in their interest. It was a decision that would weaken the power of the UN from the start.

The 'Big Three' also agreed to the rebuilding of liberated Europe and the holding of free elections: this later commitment was released as an official joint statement entitled the Declaration on Liberated Europe. On 1 March Roosevelt assured the US Congress that "we have made a start on the road to world peace". But despite Stalin's promises of democratic elections in the territories it had liberated, Soviet forces accused Poland's wartime underground leadership of being Nazi collaborators and put them on trial.

Communist governments were quickly installed in Poland and elsewhere in Eastern Europe and they would function as Soviet-controlled satellite states for decades after. Britain had gone to war with Germany in 1939 because of its treaty obligations to Poland, and the failure of Britain and the USA to ensure free elections was seen as a betrayal: many of the Poles who had fled to the West when Germany invaded, and who then fought as part of the Allied armies, refused to return home, establishing a large and still-present expatriate community in Britain.

Roosevelt died before VE Day and was succeeded as president by Harry S Truman. The new US administration soon clashed with Stalin's regime over its behaviour in Eastern Europe and its attitude to the United Nations. Within a few months the hopes that the conference guaranteed the continuation of co-operation and the sharing of goals among the Grand Alliance were dashed.

The decisions made at Yalta were controversial because they produced a divided, not united, Europe. The political and physical barriers that resulted would later famously be described by Churchill as the Iron Curtain, and presaged a new, 'cold', war. For the nations affected, the agreement to the Soviet demands were seen as a betrayal. Roosevelt and Churchill were deemed naive for accepting Stalin's promises, but their decisions were based on the need to prioritise the prosecution of the war against both Germany and Japan.

KEY BATTLE

THE VISTULA-ODER OFFENSIVE

This Soviet operation between two of Poland's great rivers in the east and west moved the frontline to the heart of the Third Reich

WORDS **PRIT BUTTAR**

Soviet tanks pictured during street fighting in Poznan, Poland

THE VISTULA-ODER OFFENSIVE

The year 1945 commenced in Europe with little doubt about how the war was going to end. In the west, the US and British forces had survived the nasty shock of Hitler's Ardennes Offensive and preparations were underway to clear the last German forces west of the Rhine before pressing into the heart of the Reich. In the east, the Red Army had swept all before it in the summer of 1944, advancing to the Vistula river, and even crossing it at three points.

It was now gathering its strength for an assault that might end the war by reaching Berlin. Most German civilians living in heavily bombed cities, exhausted by air raids and endless bad news, simply wanted the conflict to end. German soldiers awaited the renewal of enemy attacks with a mixture of fatalism and determination. Defeat seemed inevitable, but in the east there was determination to hold back the Red Army as long as possible.

They had good reason to fear the vengeance of the USSR. The loss of life in the Soviet Union during the war was on an unprecedented scale, but from the outset the German invasion had been a genocidal project. In addition to killing Jews, Gypsies and others, the plans to exploit both territory and agricultural resources would've resulted in tens of millions of Slavs dying. This was both understood and intended – the plans for exploitation of conquered territory became known as the Hunger Plan. While many of the German intentions were not accomplished, the atrocities that the Red Army uncovered as it advanced ensured that there would be a corresponding wave of violence when Soviet soldiers reached German territory. In the autumn of 1944, the Red Army briefly penetrated into East Prussia, and after the Germans recovered the village of Nemmersdorf they found many civilians had been raped, mutilated and murdered. Even if they accepted that defeat was inevitable, most German soldiers would do everything they could to hold off the Red Army in the hope that more of Germany might fall to the Western powers.

During the dark, short days of January 1945, chief of the general staff at Oberkommando des Heeres, Heinz Guderian – formerly a leading proponent of panzer warfare, now a gloomy figure struggling with increasing health problems and an utterly intransigent Führer – toured the headquarters of the formations defending Germany's Eastern Front across Poland and East Prussia. He was almost alone in the upper circles of the regime in seeing this as the most critical theatre for the Reich; after the failure of the Ardennes Offensive, Hitler remained determined to mount further attacks in the west, this time in Alsace. Some units were being sent east, but to defend Hungary, in particular to try to break the newly established Soviet encirclement of Budapest. The threat of a major Soviet attack across the open plains of Poland was ignored.

As he consulted the army group and army commanders facing this threat, Guderian's gloom must have deepened. The huge losses suffered in the summer of 1944 during the Soviet Operation Bagration, combined with the losses in northern France, meant that the frontline was held by units that were far weaker than their predecessors. Some veteran formations remained, but much of the line consisted of the new Volksgrenadier divisions, weak in numbers and perhaps more importantly experience; or improvised units cobbled together from paramilitary police formations, rear-area personnel and whoever else could be found. Senior commanders could see no prospect of defeating a major Soviet attack and had drawn up plans for a withdrawal to a shorter defence line to the west. This would release sufficient troops to establish local and area reserves, and might be sufficient to bring the expected enemy offensive to a halt. But when he returned to Hitler's headquarters to seek permission for this withdrawal, the Führer responded to Guderian's briefing by praising him for creating such a strong frontline and that no withdrawal was necessary or permitted. Guderian retorted that the Eastern Front was no more than a house of cards and would collapse at the first blow.

It is a measure of the delusional mindset of Hitler and his inner circle that they chose to believe what they wanted to be true. The Red Army, they posited, had lost so many men in the preceding years that it must be at the end of its strength – the clear preparations for a new offensive were no more than a gigantic bluff. But the reality was very different. Despite its losses, the Red Army intended to continue its thrusts into Hungary and the Balkans, but was deploying its main strength for what it regarded as the most important axis: the direct route to Berlin across Poland. There were several reasons for this. First, Stalin wished to capture Silesia as soon as possible; it was an industrial region that was vital for Germany's munitions production and its loss would hasten the final collapse of the Reich. Second, despite agreements with the Western powers, Stalin continued to fear that the British and Americans might make a separate peace with Hitler. It was therefore vital to reach Berlin as soon as possible, and the greatest concentration of Soviet forces would be for an offensive from the Vistula towards the west.

The assault that Guderian feared would be launched primarily by two Fronts. In the south, General Ivan Stepanovich Konev's 1st Ukrainian Front had seized a large bridgehead across the Vistula near Sandomierz, and had spent the winter turning it into a huge armed camp. Konev had 1.2 million soldiers, 3,600 tanks and assault guns and more than 17,000 guns and mortars, supported by over 2,500 aircraft. This was far

As the Red Army pushed west, its soldiers inflicted brutal reprisals on German civilians

Soviet troops pose next to a crashed German aircraft after the end of the war, Wroclaw, Poland

Red Army soldiers during street fighting in Poznan, Poland

"FOR 90 MINUTES, SOVIET SHELLS CHURNED UP THE GROUND IN ONE OF THE HEAVIEST BOMBARDMENTS OF THE WAR. ALMOST EVERY GERMAN POSITION WAS HIT REPEATEDLY"

greater than the combined strength of all German units deployed across Poland and East Prussia, but was only part of the Red Army's force.

To the north, Marshal Georgi Konstantinovich Zhukov's 1st Belarusian Front occupied two smaller bridgeheads to the south of Warsaw, at Magnuszew and Puławy. His total strength was similar to that of Konev, but the limited space in his bridgeheads meant that his exploitation forces would have to wait on the east bank of the Vistula. At the same time as breaking out of these two bridgeheads, Zhukov's Front would seize a new crossing point north of Warsaw, and inevitably these factors would slow the advance. To make matters worse for the Germans, two further Fronts would attack further north into East Prussia, tying down any German units in that area.

Soviet accounts often suggest that the timing of the offensive was brought forward at the request of the Western Allies to force the Germans to abandon the Ardennes Offensive, but this is simply untrue. The tide turned against the Germans in the Ardennes before the end of 1944, and many German units had already been withdrawn by 12 January, when Konev commenced his assault. As was usually the case, the offensive started with an artillery bombardment followed by aggressive 'reconnaissance in force'. This proved to be stronger than in the past, and the Germans believed that this was the main attack. As firing slackened, some hoped that they had fended off the Soviet attack, but then Konev's artillery spoke again. For 90 minutes, shells churned up the ground in one of the heaviest bombardments of the war. In earlier offensives, Soviet artillery preparation had often been heavy but imprecise, leaving many German positions intact. On this occasion, almost every German position was hit repeatedly. When they advanced, the soldiers of 1st Ukrainian Front found shattered trenches and bunkers and rapidly overwhelmed the German survivors. By the end of 12 January, Konev's two tank armies were moving forward. Guderian's prediction had been correct: the house of cards had collapsed at the first blow.

Zhukov's offensive started on 14 January. Here too, the initial artillery bombardment was brutal. The powerful reconnaissance in force was more successful than expected and the

German POWs in Wroclaw, Poland, March 1945

THE VISTULA-ODER OFFENSIVE

Heinz Guderian's warnings of a Soviet offensive in Poland went largely ignored by Hitler

Ivan Konev's powerful 1st Ukrainian Front overmatched the combined German forces in Poland and East Prussia

main artillery preparation around the Puławy bridgehead was cancelled. As a consequence of having to advance from two small bridgeheads and perhaps due to this decision not to conduct a full bombardment, Zhukov's forces made slower progress than Konev's units in the south. Nevertheless, the operation was off to a good start. The Germans had anticipated Soviet attacks from the Vistula bridgeheads and had positioned their modest armoured assets accordingly, with the intention of carrying out rapid counterattacks against both Konev's and Zhukov's armies. In the south, Hitler had insisted that the two panzer divisions were held close to the frontline, and consequently they were caught in the initial Soviet bombardment and air attacks. They had to wait for permission from Hitler's headquarters before they could go into action, by which time any chance of success was gone.

Oberst Albert Brux, commander of 17th Panzer Division, was taken prisoner when Soviet units overwhelmed his headquarters. The neighbouring 16th Panzer Division fared a little better, but could do nothing to stop the torrent of Soviet armour pouring west. To the north, Zhukov's units also faced two panzer divisions. One of these, 19th Panzer Division, ran into the Soviet Eighth Guards Army that was advancing out of the Magnuszew bridgehead and was brought to a halt by Soviet anti-tank guns that had been deployed rapidly to cover such a counterattack. A little to the north, 25th Panzer Division fared a little better, denting the advance of the Soviet Fifth Shock Army, but any German successes were modest. By 16 January the entire frontline was disintegrating and Soviet units were racing west.

The days that followed saw a series of running battles. Substantial German forces had been left stranded near Kielce, and rather than attempt to establish a firm encirclement, the Soviet units simply left them for the second echelon to crush. Was this a mistake? Under the command of the capable General Walther Nehring, these German units succeeded in making their way west, fighting only when necessary. Ultimately, Nehring led his men to a link-up with German units that were attempting to restore the frontline and these formations would play parts in the last battles of the Reich, but they could do little to change the outcome of the fighting across Poland, and a tighter encirclement might have delayed the Soviet tank armies from pushing so far west. Reinforcements were dispatched from East Prussia but arrived piecemeal and were barely sufficient to rescue Nehring and his units; meanwhile, fresh Soviet attacks burst into East Prussia, where the defences had been fatally weakened by these transfers.

After the war, Sergei Matveevich Shtemenko, head of the Soviet Operations Directorate, wrote that it would've been unrealistic to plan for a single operation that would carry the Red Army from the Vistula to Berlin and beyond. As the Soviet armies approached the line of the Oder and Neisse rivers, they were running out of momentum – losses had been substantial and, more importantly, it was proving difficult to move supplies forward across the devastated landscape of Poland. After a rapid advance across the frozen country, vehicles were now becoming stranded in muddy conditions as the weather grew warmer. Some – notably Vasily Ivanovich Chuikov, who had commanded the defence of Stalingrad and whose Eighth Guards Army was in the forefront of Zhukov's assault – suggested in their memoirs that continuing across the Oder to Berlin, while risky, might have been successful. But this is surely incorrect.

The Germans could be expected to fight hard for their capital, and success would be more likely if the Red Army paused and gathered its strength. On the other side of the frontline, whether it was fanaticism or weary fatalism, there seemed no way out of the conflict for most Germans. Belief in Hitler and the Nazi Party was far from the delirious heights of earlier years, but despite the evidence on all sides, it remained strong in some parts of both civilian and military life. For the rest of Germany, there was a sense of hopelessness and of being trapped in a disaster that grew worse by the day and that would continue for a further few weeks. Hitler was still alive, and – one way or another – he remained an insurmountable obstacle to peace, even the peace of utter defeat.

A Soviet tank and troops of the 1st Ukrainian Front on a street in Gleiwitz, German Silesia

KEY TECH
WILLYS JEEP

The most iconic light transport vehicle of World War II, the Willys jeep was versatile, manoeuvrable and fast over uneven terrain

WORDS **MICHAEL E. HASKEW**

The first and most distinctive jeep ever built, the Willys jeep was designed in 1940 as part of a competition to provide the US Army with a new light transport vehicle for the impending World War II. It dictated light transport vehicle design for decades to come, only being phased out in the late Seventies. Light, adaptable and highly manoeuvrable, the Willys jeep in its various forms (MA, MB and post-war M38/M606) allowed allied forces to transport troops, munitions and injured soldiers to and from the front line quickly.

Central to its effectiveness was its L134 2.2-litre engine, capable of producing 60hp at 4,000rpm. This granted the lightweight Willys (1,040kg) a top speed of 45mph and earned the engine the nickname of 'Go Devil' by Allied troops. The engine was controlled by a Warner T-84J three-speed synchromesh transmission, which provided three forward gears and one in reverse in a four-wheel drive setup. Importantly, this enabled the jeep to easily traverse road, desert, scrub and jungle terrain.

The engine was forward-mounted to a lightweight steel chassis. This featured a foldable windscreen, slatted iron grille (later additions included a steel grated grille), and front frame cross-member for rigidity and damage mitigation. The chassis sat on top of a compact 80-inch wheelbase that was installed with leaf springs and shock absorbers (excellent for passage over bumpy ground), as well as fully hydraulic brakes on each of its four wheels (granting fantastic stopping power).

The Willys jeep was also prized for its high adaptability, with various different vehicle setups possible dependent on the mission role in question. Troop transport maximised passenger space, with extra seats at the rear, while as a mobile medical centre the rear seats could be removed to make way for stretchers, medicines and operating equipment. The jeep could also be installed with various weapons platforms, including a rear-mounted 37mm cannon and array of different Browning M1917 machine guns.

After the end of the Second World War, the Willys jeep was subsequently upgraded with a larger engine (the F4-134 Hurricane), more durable transmission (Warner T-90) and a range of advanced instrumentation and electronics. Nonetheless it was eventually replaced in the late Seventies and early Eighties as larger, more armoured vehicles like the Humvee became the military's primary troop transporters.

WILLYS JEEP

CREW 3
CAPACITY 5
WEIGHT 1,040 KG (2,293LB)
LENGTH 3.3 METRES (131 INCHES)
WIDTH 1.57 METRES (62 INCHES)
HEIGHT 1.83 METRES (72 INCHES)
ENGINE 4-CYLINDER, 2.2-LITRE L134 PETROL
MAX HORSEPOWER 60HP @ 4,000RPM
MAX SPEED 45MPH (72.4KPH)
TRANSMISSION WARNER T-84J 3-SPEED SYNCHROMESH
PRODUCED 640,000

The Willys' versatility was its greatest asset, allowing it to be used in a variety of roles

> "THE WILLYS JEEP WAS PRIZED FOR ITS HIGH ADAPTABILITY, WITH VARIOUS DIFFERENT SETUPS POSSIBLE DEPENDENT ON MISSION ROLE"

WILLYS JEEP

US soldiers march alongside a Willys jeep towing a trailer

UNDER THE HOOD
THE COMPONENTS THAT MADE UP THIS EFFECTIVE WAR VEHICLE

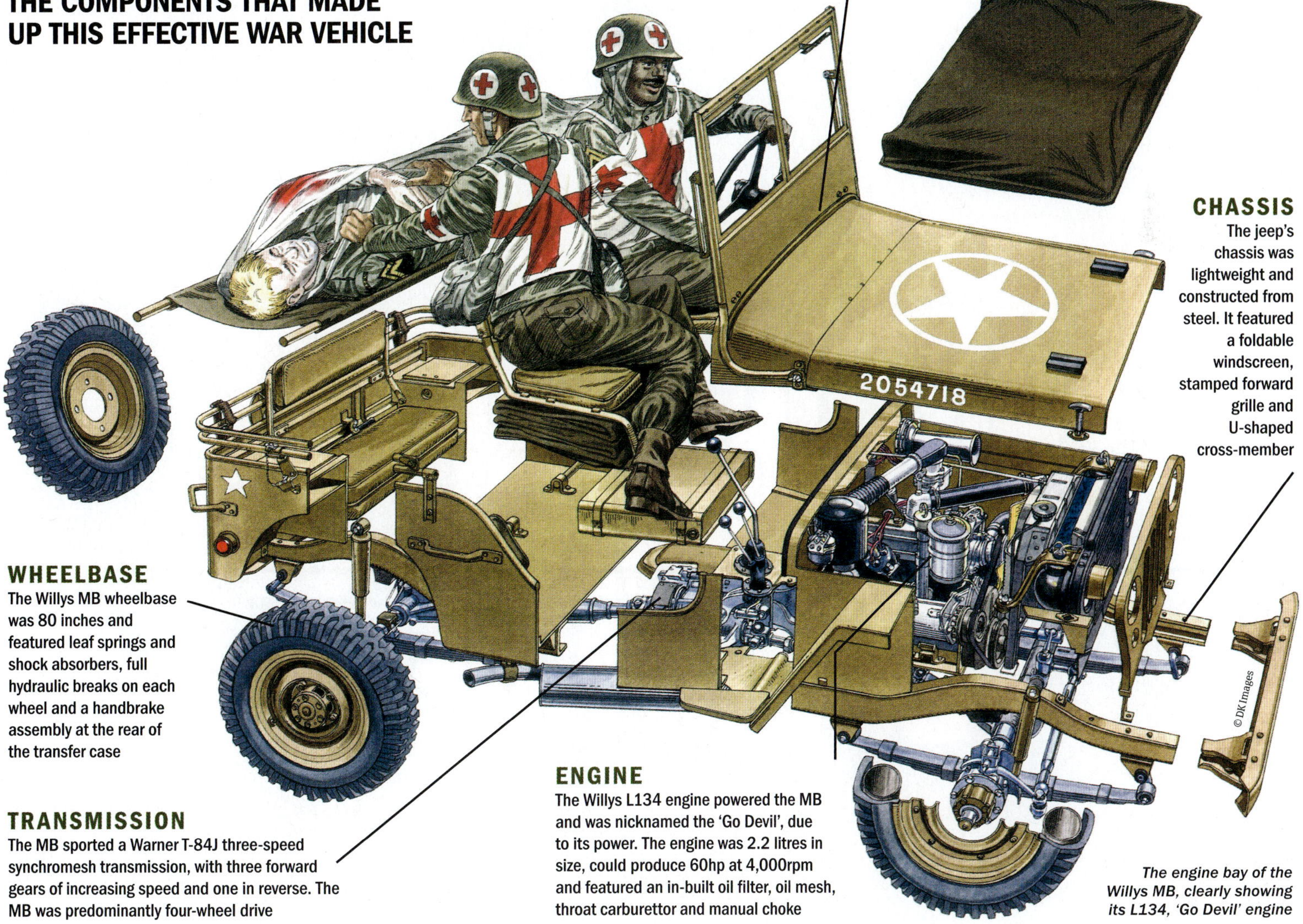

INSTRUMENTATION
The Willys MB jeep was fitted with a 0-60 mph speedometer, 0-220 Fahrenheit temperature gauge, oil pressure monitor and map light

CHASSIS
The jeep's chassis was lightweight and constructed from steel. It featured a foldable windscreen, stamped forward grille and U-shaped cross-member

WHEELBASE
The Willys MB wheelbase was 80 inches and featured leaf springs and shock absorbers, full hydraulic breaks on each wheel and a handbrake assembly at the rear of the transfer case

TRANSMISSION
The MB sported a Warner T-84J three-speed synchromesh transmission, with three forward gears of increasing speed and one in reverse. The MB was predominantly four-wheel drive

ENGINE
The Willys L134 engine powered the MB and was nicknamed the 'Go Devil', due to its power. The engine was 2.2 litres in size, could produce 60hp at 4,000rpm and featured an in-built oil filter, oil mesh, throat carburettor and manual choke

The engine bay of the Willys MB, clearly showing its L134, 'Go Devil' engine

★ 4 MAY 1945 ★

LÜNEBURG HEATH INSTRUMENT OF SURRENDER

The first German surrender of 1945 was made to British Field Marshal Bernard Montgomery

LÜNEBURG HEATH INSTRUMENT OF SURRENDER

Montgomery signs the instrument of surrender at Lüneburg Heath.

Field Marshal Bernard Montgomery received the unconditional surrender of the German forces in northwest Europe within his mobile headquarters on the heather-covered hills of Lüneburg Heath. The surrender included troops in the Netherlands, northwest Germany (and its islands), and Denmark, as well as all the naval vessels in this area.

The new Fuhrer after Hitler's death, Grand Admiral Karl Dönitz, was not present at the negotiations or surrender ceremony, believing discussions with a field marshal were beneath him. A plan of the intended Allied occupation zones had fallen into German hands. Dönitz ordered his representatives to buy as much time as possible, ensure any surrender was localised and guarantee a pocket of the west bank of the Elbe to provide sanctuary from the Soviet occupation zone. Montgomery did not humour any such attempts during negotiations on 3 May. He demanded the unconditional surrender of all the forces his men faced and refused to negotiate the fate of the remaining German troops until the capitulation. Dönitz accepted Montgomery's terms.

Admiral Hans-Georg von Friedeburg (Oberbefehlshaber der Kriegsmarine), General Eberhard Kinzel (Army Group Weichsel), Rear Admiral Gerhard Wagner (Kriegsmarine staff), Colonel Fritz Poleck (Oberkommando der Wehrmacht), and Major Hans Jochen Friedel (Kinzel's staff officer) signed on 4 May. The instrument of surrender bears a single Allied signature: Montgomery.

KEY BATTLE

BATTLE OF BERLIN

During the final days of the Third Reich, the heart of its capital became 'Objective 105' for the Red Army, and the fight to take it saw some of the fiercest clashes in the wider struggle for the city

WORDS ANTHONY TUCKER-JONES

The Soviet Red Banner is hoisted over the Reichstag in the iconic staged photo

BATTLE OF BERLIN

For the Red Army the most symbolic objective in Berlin was the imposing Reichstag, Germany's former parliament building on the eastern side of the vast square known as the Königsplatz. Joseph Stalin himself had chosen this as his army's main goal rather than the Reich Chancellery, where Adolf Hitler's bunker lay. The ruined Reichstag had suffered an arson attack just four weeks after Hitler came to power in 1933. During the war it was employed as a hospital. As far as Stalin was concerned, once the hammer and sickle flag was raised over the Reichstag it would signal an end to the battle for Berlin. Whoever was first to get the 'Victory Banner' in place would become a Hero of the Soviet Union. As an incentive, nine of these banners were issued to the assault divisions of the 3rd Shock Army.

When the Red Army launched its infantry assault on the city on 21 April 1945, the artillery bombardment further damaged the building. Shells crashed through the enormous cupola, bringing down some of the girders supporting it. Six days later at 2pm it was shelled by the 347th Guards Heavy Self-Propelled Artillery Regiment deployed in Charlottenburg.

The honour of storming what Marshal Zhukov's planners had dubbed 'Objective 105' was assigned to Major General Perevertkin's 79th Rifle Corps. This consisted of the 150th, 171st and 207th Rifle Divisions, each with three rifle regiments. The western section of the Reichstag was to be assaulted by Major General Shatilov's 150th Division, while Colonel Negoda's 171st Division attacked the eastern side. It would be no easy task and Perevertkin was reinforced with artillery, self-propelled guns and tanks. First, though, his men had to get over the river Spree, in the face of determined German opposition.

'Himmler's House'

Negoda's division was ordered to seize the Moltke bridge, which gave access to the Königsplatz via Moltkestrasse. They were then to clear the German strongpoint on the corner of Moltkestrasse and Kronprinzenufer, which dominated the approaches to the bridge. Afterwards Negoda's men were to join Shatilov's division in taking Objective 107 – the vast Ministry of Internal Affairs known as 'Himmler's House'. This was located on the southern side of Moltkestrasse and its capture would put Soviet troops in position to directly assault the Reichstag itself across the open reaches of the Königsplatz. They were supported by the 23rd Tank Brigade commanded by Lieutenant Colonel Morozov, Lieutenant General Kirichenko's 9th Tank Corps, and the 10th Independent Flamethrower Battalion. Shatilov's men on Negoda's right flank first had to clear the defenders from the Custom Yard to the west of the bridge before they could cross. On Negoda's left flank Colonel Asafov's 207th Division was to clear the imposing Lehrter railway station.

Soviet forces pictured next to the battle-scarred Brandenburg Gate

The Germans were expecting the Soviets to force a crossing, so the Moltke bridge was well defended. On the northern bank they had built extensive barricades around it along the Alt Moabitstrasse. They also barricaded themselves in the Customs Yard and the Lehrter Station – the latter was held by elements of the 9th Parachute Division. The bridge itself was covered in barbed-wire and mines, the southern exit was blocked by heaped rubble and steel girders, and the southern bank had been fortified with pill-boxes. 'Himmler's House' was held by a mixture of SS units under the command of a police colonel, while two infantry companies from the SS Anhalt Regiment were deployed either side supported by 250 sailors.

In the stronghold on the corner of Alt Moabit and Kronprinzenufer, SS-Sergeant Major Willi Rogmann set up an observation post for his mortar platoon, as did Sergeant Major Kurt Abicht for his artillery battery. Their weaponry comprised just two mortars and two guns that were deployed to cover the bridge.

German troops in the buildings lining Schlieffenufer, which ran along the southern bank west of the bridge, were able to support the Customs Yard and fire on the northern approaches to the bridge. The defenders could also call on support from the Luftwaffe's heavy guns on the Zoo flak tower and guns in the Tiergarten.

On the evening of 28 April Soviet tanks stormed the northern barricades protecting the Moltke bridge, thrusting along Alt Moabit and toward the Customs Yard, but the supporting riflemen were driven back when they came in range of the pill-boxes' machine guns. Just after midnight two battalions from the 380th Rifle and the

Below: The shattered remains of the Reichstag, pictured on 6 July 1945

Red Army troops advance on the Reichstag in the last hours of the fighting

A Soviet soldier is photographed next to the corpse of a German

756th Rifle Regiments from the 171st and 150th Divisions stormed over the bridge. However, the Germans remained holding the fortified corner buildings and these had to be cleared before the Spree could be forced in strength. Zhukov recalled: "In the Reichstag district the enemy resisted our advancing troops desperately, having turned every building, stairway, room, cellar into strongpoints and defensive positions." Once the 380th and 756th Regiments were over the river they were followed by the 171st Division's 525th Regiment, which moved northeast into the Diplomatic Quarter.

On the northern bank men of the 9th Parachute Division launched a surprise counterattack. Remarkably, in the confusion 100 Germans were able to fight their way over the bridge to safety. This combined with a German counterattack on the southern bank briefly threw the Soviet bridgehead into chaos. Now that the Soviet assault groups were overwhelming the northern perimeter, the Germans attempted to drop the bridge into the Spree. They had rigged it with explosives and when these were detonated the entire area vanished into a cloud of dust and smoke. When this cleared it showed that the bridge, although damaged, was still standing and passable to vehicles.

'Himmler's House' was bombarded for ten minutes from 7am on 29 April and was soon in flames. After capturing the corner of Alt Moabit and Kronprinzenufer, the Soviets hauled mortars up to the second floor and fired at the ministry from there too. The blaze caused a great pall of smoke which obscured the Soviets' view down Moltkestrasse toward the Reichstag. From 8.30am Soviet guns and rocket launchers deluged the defensive positions around the Reichstag for 90 minutes. In retaliation, the Zoo flak tower's guns hit Soviet artillery and self-propelled guns that were firing across the river from the captured Customs Yard. However, the Soviets quickly brought forward replacements.

Heavy fighting followed and by noon the Soviet 380th and 756th Regiments had forced their way into the courtyard of the Ministry of Internal Affairs. The Germans continued resisting on the first floor, where Soviet riflemen secured a few rooms. Shatilov had to deploy reinforcements in the shape of the 674th Rifle Regiment to take the south-western corner of the ministry, and it took until 4.30am to finally overcome the last of the stubborn German defenders. During that time the 171st Division cleared the western half of the Diplomatic Quarter. "Now we're tightening the circle round the centre of the city," wrote Soviet soldier Vladimir Pereverzev. "I am just 500 metres

"FOR THE NEXT 90 MINUTES SOVIET GUNS AND ROCKET LAUNCHERS DELUGED THE DEFENSIVE POSITIONS AROUND THE REICHSTAG"

The survivors of Berlin's defeated garrison are marched into captivity

BATTLE OF BERLIN

Soviet gunners shell German positions at close range

Triumphant Soviet troops outside the blazing Reichstag

Katyusha rocket launchers hammer Berlin's defences

[1,640ft] from the Reichstag… We'll be in the Reichstag tomorrow."

In the meantime, Soviet tanks had rolled over the Moltke bridge, some of which stopped on the southern bank to shell German positions still on the other side of the river. The Soviet armour included Stalin heavy tanks armed with a powerful 4.8in (122mm) gun, which were used to fire into the surrounding buildings at point-blank range. This progress, though, had come at a price as German anti-tank guns and soldiers armed with Panzerfausts ensured that the Alt Moabit and Moltkestrasse were left littered with wrecked Soviet tanks. Two T-34 medium tanks reached the end of Moltekestrasse and were in sight of the Reichstag when they were hit and caught fire. The second tank threw its tracks before clattering to a halt. When the crews emerged and tried to escape they were shot down in the street.

Bitter fighting

The 150th and 171st Rifle Divisions made their final preparations to assault the Reichstag on the morning of 30 April. In Moscow, Red Army Chief of Operations General SM Shtemenko was delighted by the news. "In Berlin, there was fighting close to the Reichstag and the Reich Chancellery," he reported, "which for several days had been under constant and accurate fire from Soviet infantry and artillery." That day Zhukov's intelligence assessed: "The Reichstag… was defended by crack SS units. In the early hours on 28 April, 1945, the enemy parachuted in a battalion of marines to reinforce the defences of the district." According to Zhukov's intelligence the Reichstag district was held by almost 6,000 troops supported by artillery, assault guns and panzers.

After the fall of the Moltke bridge and the Ministry of Internal Affairs, the Germans defending the Reichstag were waiting for the Red Army to press home its attack. A mixture of troops held the Königsplatz, including a Luftwaffe flak battery that had a few 3.5in (88mm) guns, one of which had white bands painted round the barrel indicating it had destroyed 16 aircraft or tanks.

This particular gun was positioned to fire up the Moltkestrasse and although it was screened by a row of abandoned vehicles, it was not dug in, leaving the crew exposed. The German defenders also had panzers concealed to the right of the Reichstag. Forces deployed in the surrounding streets were ordered to counterattack at the earliest opportunity.

No matter how much firepower the Red Army poured into the Königsplatz it would still be a difficult space to cross without suffering heavy casualties. Soviet war correspondent Vassili Subbotin observed: "It seemed impassable, covered with shell holes, railway sleepers, pieces of wire and trenches." Shatilov, commander of the 150th Division, allotted 'Victory Banner' No 5 to Colonel Zinchenko's 756th Regiment. Zinchenko in turn issued it to Captain Neustroyev's 1st Battalion. Captain Davydov's 1st Battalion, 674th Regiment, Senior Lieutenant Samsonov's 1st Battalion, 380th Regiment, and two assault teams from the 79th Rifle Corps command under Major Bondar and Captain Makov were also assigned banners. Everyone was eager to plant their flag and make history.

"Permission to be the first to break into the Reichstag with my section?" Sergeant Ishchanov asked Captain Neustroyev in 'Himmler's House'. Neustroyev nodded in agreement and at 6am Ishchanov's men clambered out of a first-floor window and made their way onto the Königsplatz. "Suddenly a soldier rose up, unfolded a red flag and charged forward," wrote Subbotin. "That was Pyotr Pyatnizki." In the middle they and the other attackers were impeded by the water obstacle.

German crossfire coming from the Reichstag on the eastern side of the Königsplatz and the Kroll Opera House on western side swept the square mercilessly. Fresh Soviet troops were ordered to clear the opera house. The German flak guns on the Zoo bunker firing from 1.2 miles (2km) away also added to the carnage. "Again there was a well-known whizzing sound over us, and heavy shells ripped up the asphalt," reported Subbotin. When the assault battalion from the 380th Regiment reached the northwest corner of the Reichstag they came under immediate counterattack by German tanks, and a Soviet anti-tank battalion was called to deal with them. "On this day, it was one of the most strenuous days of the war," said Subbotin. "There was bitter fighting on the square in front of the Reichstag."

Meanwhile the Red Army moved artillery, tanks and rocket launchers across the Moltke bridge in growing numbers. However, it was still under fire from German troops in the Schlieffenufer buildings and the Tiergarten. Asafov's 207th Division was ordered to clear the Schlieffenufer before pushing south to take the opera house. Once across the river the guns of the Soviet 420th Anti-Tank Artillery Division were manhandled onto the roof of 'Himmler's House' and ten rocket launchers were positioned in its courtyard.

Tanks and artillery were also gathered at the end of Moltkestrasse opposite the Swiss embassy. At 1pm the Soviets deployed 89 guns, plus Katyusha rocket launchers, to pound the defenders of the Reichstag for 30 minutes. Many of the bricked-up windows at the front of the Reichstag were blasted open by direct fire, and under this covering barrage the assault battalions crept closer.

'Off you go, lads'

Neustroyev's reconnaissance troop with their banner, along with the advance company, entered the Reichstag via the doors and breaches in the walls. His men were photographed dashing towards the building but this was probably a re-enactment for the benefit of Soviet cameramen. Reaching the central staircase, they cleared the first floor, but not before the Germans hurled grenades down the stairs, showering deadly shrapnel everywhere. When the Soviets reached the second floor, Sergeants Kantaria and Yegorov drove the defenders back using grenades. They prematurely raised their banner No 5 over the ruined staircase at 2.25pm, only to be halted on the third floor by intense machine gun fire.

Neustoyev put Lieutenant Berest in charge of the assault group and tasked him with clearing the second floor. Colonel Zinchenko in the meantime greeted Kantaria and Yegorov, who had retrieved their Victory Banner, with a smile. "Well then, off you go, lads," he said and then, pointing upwards, added: "And stick the banner up there." Zhukov recalled: "However, even after the lower storeys of the Reichstag had been taken, the enemy garrison did not surrender. Fierce fighting took place inside the building." A renewed push to secure the Reichstag was launched at 6pm. Meanwhile the 171st Rifle Division fought to clear the rest of the Diplomatic Quarter to the north of the Königsplatz. It also moved to secure the Kronprinzen Bridge over the Spree to ensure no German reinforcements could reach the Diplomatic Quarter.

It took almost four hours of bitter close-quarter combat before the banner was eventually hung

> "THE SECOND TANK THREW ITS TRACKS BEFORE CLATTERING TO A HALT. WHEN THE CREWS EMERGED AND TRIED TO ESCAPE THEY WERE SHOT DOWN IN THE STREET"

Below: Soviet tank and anti-tank gun on the approaches to the Reichstag

BATTLE OF BERLIN

Soviet troops who stormed the Reichstag pose with their banner

Photos of celebrating Red Army soldiers were seen by millions of Russian civilians back home

above the building. "At 9.50pm on April 30, Sergeant MA Yegorov and Junior Sergeant MV Kantaria hoisted the Victory Flag received from the army Military Council on the main cupola of the Reichstag," recounted Zhukov. Some Soviet gunners had beaten the two sergeants to it, but as Soviet photographer Yevgeni Khaldei was not ready their efforts were considered unofficial.

The now world-famous staged photo was taken two days later. "Not until evening as the Sun began to set, lighting up the entire horizon with its red glow, did two of our soldiers raise the banner of victory on the burned-out cupola," wrote General Perevertkin. General Kuznetsov called Zhukov to report: "The Red Flag is on the Reichstag! Hurrah, Comrade Marshal!"

Zhukov later wrote with huge satisfaction: "Finally I received the long-awaited call from Kuznetzov, the Reichstag had been taken; our red banner had been planted on it and was waving from the building." Zhukov was understandably elated and added as an afterthought: "What a stream of thoughts raced through my mind at that joyous moment!"

Nonetheless, even then the Red Army had not overcome all of the German garrison. Deep in the bowels of the Reichstag some 300 Soviet riflemen found themselves battling to contain a much larger force of German troops who refused to give up. "The cellars were full of fascists," said Rifleman Pyotr Schtscherbina. "They threw hand grenades and fired Panzerfausts at us, dust falling from above. But we stood at the cellar entrances and fired back."

Elsewhere in the building German stragglers prowled along the corridors catching unwary Soviet soldiers. No mercy was shown or expected by either side. Both resorted to pistols and knives. "The fighting within the main building of the Reichstag repeatedly took the form of hand-to-hand combat," observed Zhukov.

Surrender or burn

Sheltering in the southwestern cellars of the Reichstag were survivors of the Luftwaffe flak battery, who had escaped from their positions on the Königsplatz. They had not been involved in the defence of the building on 30 April, but the following day took part in an unsuccessful counterattack. The gunners had been so cocooned that they did not realise the Soviets were above them until ordered into action. The fighting in the cellars continued until the afternoon of 1 May, when the exhausted defenders announced they wished to lay down their arms. This was prompted by parts of the building being on fire. "It was hot," recalled Rifleman Schtscherbina. "The building filled with smoke. The fire soon reached us and we could no longer stay." Furthermore, communication with Babick had been cut by this point.

Captain Neustroyev, Lieutenant Berest and a translator went to negotiate. They were greeted by three officers and a female translator. The Germans mistook Berest for a colonel so spoke with him. "We have not come to Berlin to let you monsters go," warned Berest. "If you do not surrender, not one of you here will come out alive."

The Germans wanted the Soviet troops to parade outside in front of the Reichstag so there would be no misunderstanding when they came out. Affronted, Berest refused and with Neustroyev and their interpreter left.

The trapped defenders surrendered later that night. The Soviets discovered that the basement held 300 German soldiers, 500 wounded and 200 dead. "Only individual groups of Nazis in different sections of the Reichstag cellar continued to resist until the morning on May 2," said Zhukov. Soviet troops, weary of fighting by torchlight, resorted to using flamethrowers to silence the last of the recalcitrant resistance. Those who refused to give in were incinerated.

The Soviets suffered heavy losses – 2,200 dead – in the battle to take the Reichstag. After storming the building, Senior Sergeant Ilya Syanov's company was reduced from 83 men to 26, and when the survivors emerged, Syanov observed: "The soldiers looked awful, with burns and other wounds. Their coats were torn, their shoes burnt through, and from their boots jutted the rags and tatters of their footcloths." General Perevertkin claimed his corps killed 2,500 Germans and captured 2,600; however, such numbers were far greater than the actual garrison of the area. By this stage Hitler was dead and Berlin had fallen.

A German veteran and young boy brace themselves for an attack by the Red Army

Marshal Zhukov was told his primary objective in Berlin was the Reichstag

Wilhelm Keitel (centre) at the signing of the unconditional surrender in Berlin.

UNCONDITIONAL SURRENDER IN REIMS AND BERLIN

★ 8-9 MAY 1945 ★

UNCONDITIONAL SURRENDER IN REIMS AND BERLIN

The Western and Eastern allies laid down their terms for total victory in Europe

From 6 May, Eisenhower began demanding Germany's immediate and unconditional surrender on all fronts. Dönitz dispatched General Alfred Jodl, hoping to buy time. The General had no meaningful discussions with Eisenhower, who announced that he would close British and American lines to surrendering Germans.

The prospect of fighting Germans losing their soldier status was enough for Dönitz to agree to the terms. General Jodl signed the first of two total unconditional surrenders in the Collège Moderne et Technique de Reims that had been serving as Supreme Headquarters Allied Expeditionary Force (SHAEF).

The Soviet High Command refused to accept the Reims agreement. It wanted to sign an unconditional surrender at the seat of German power, Berlin, that fully recognised the Soviets' contribution. Eisenhower agreed to these demands, positioning Reims as a temporary ceasefire before the main unconditional surrender. The Berlin capitulation was signed for the Allies by Arthur Tedder (RAF) and Georgy Zhukov. Hans-Georg von Friedeburg, Wilhelm Keitel and Hans-Jürgen Stumpff signed on Nazi Germany's behalf. French and US witnesses were also present.

Many reporters watched the Reims surrender, but were under an embargo that was extended once it became clear that a second agreement involving the Soviets was needed. However, the Associated Press' Edward Kennedy broke the embargo on 7 May, and the surrender soon made headlines worldwide. The Western Allies celebrated VE Day on 8 May, while the Soviets waited until 9 May to observe Victory Day. Meanwhile, the Associated Press fired Kennedy and apologised to his family 67 years later.

Allied commanders (left to right) Ivan Susloparov, Frederick E Morgan, Walter Bedell Smith, Harry Butcher, Eisenhower and Arthur Tedder celebrate the Reims surrender.

KEY BATTLE

BURMA CAMPAIGN

While WWII was drawing to a close in Europe, teenage British soldier Jim Kemp was still experiencing a vicious campaign in the jungles of Burma

WORDS **TOM GARNER**

BURMA CAMPAIGN

As the guns fell silent over Europe on VE Day in May 1945, the momentous news meant virtually nothing to Allied soldiers who were fighting on the far side of the world. Campaigning in hot, humid conditions against an enemy who had no concept of surrender, the British Fourteenth Army in Burma could only wish to put down their weapons. The Imperial Japanese Army would fight to the death and in the end it would take the use of nuclear weapons on home soil to force their capitulation.

By 1945 Britain's Fourteenth Army had pushed the Japanese back to the very gates of the Burmese capital. Dubbed the 'Forgotten Army' by the press and even their own redoubtable commander, this force was nevertheless characterised by great bravery and military success under truly terrible conditions.

Among their number from early 1945 was a teenage British conscript called Jim Kemp who fought with the army during its final push against the Japanese. Speaking in 2020, 75 years after VJ Day was finally declared, Kemp described his experiences of jungle warfare, hand-to-hand combat and the traumatic birth of modern India.

Ramree Island

By January 1945, the Fourteenth Army was advancing upon the Burmese capital of Rangoon (now Yangon), which was located on the Southern Front of the campaign. Allied operations were not just conducted inland but also on the Burmese coast, which included the Japanese-occupied Ramree Island. Located off the shores of what is now Rakhine State, Ramree is the largest island off Burma, although it is only separated by a thin strait of approximately 150 metres in width.

In January 1945, the island was occupied by a Japanese garrison that included a battalion from 121st Infantry Regiment. The British wanted to retake Ramree so that they could establish airbases to support the mainland campaign. Lieutenant-General William Slim, Commander of the Fourteenth Army, considered that Ramree "would provide the sea-supplied airfields that could nourish my army in a dash for Rangoon".

The Japanese had already established an airfield, which needed to be captured and on 14 January the 26th Indian Infantry Division was ordered to conduct an amphibious assault under the command of Major-General Cyril Lomax. With naval and air support, the British had to first capture the port of Kyaukpyu in the northern part of the island, as well as the nearby airfield.

For Kemp, who was still only 19 by this stage, Ramree Island would be his first experience of combat, "The Japanese had been on there for quite a while and they'd built a big airfield. The British decided that they didn't want the Japanese to bomb or shoot at our boys so our first task was to get rid of the airfield."

Assault troops were deployed to land on beaches west of Kyaukpyu with the amphibious landings being codenamed 'Operation Matador'. For the young Kemp, his introduction to warfare included simplistic orders, "The attack was well planned and organised,"he recalled. "They basically said to us boys, 'The airfield is over there about five miles away – in you go and sort it out'. That was it."

Kyaukpyu and the nearby airfield were taken but the Japanese continued to fight rear-guard actions in the forests and swamps of Ramree for weeks afterwards until the island was secured on 17 February. Kemp understatedly recalls that the battle and the fighting he experienced elsewhere in Burma was always confusing and uncertain, "What an experience that was! In those days you didn't know where you were going, what you were going to do or whether you could do it. A lot of the time the fighting that awaited us was an unknown quantity and we didn't know if we were going to come back again. The Japanese on Ramree Island were pretty resilient and they would rather have been killed than surrender, put it that way."

Operation Dracula

After Ramree Island, the Warwicks moved back to mainland Burma and began preparing for the capture of Rangoon itself. As well as being the Burmese capital, Rangoon was the main seaport for the Japanese to receive supplies and reinforcements. Its strategic importance had already been demonstrated when the Japanese had bombed the city in December 1941, which caused much of its population to flee.

Left without an effective administration, British-led Allied forces could not hold Rangoon from the Japanese invasion in March 1942 and they had been compelled to evacuate from the capital. This had serious consequences because the fall of Rangoon meant that the Allies could no longer defend Burma and were forced to retreat to India and parts of China.

By early 1945, the situation had been reversed but with more severe ramifications for the Japanese. The Allies had already taken Mandalay and Meiktila and the Japanese could not advance either to the north or east from Rangoon because it would cut their links to the Burma Railway. The railway had been built at the cost of 102,000 Allied prisoners-of-war who died during its construction but it was the vital Japanese supply link between Burma and their occupied territories

British soldiers pictured during mopping-up operations at Pyawbwe during the advance on Rangoon

in Thailand and Malaya. If Rangoon fell to the Allies, the Japanese would be forced to withdraw from most of Burma. They would also have to abandon much of their equipment because a retreat would require a march on foot through thick jungle.

From April 1945, the Fourteenth Army advanced to within 40 miles of Rangoon but they became delayed by a Japanese force at Pegu (now Bago). This delay was a concern to the Allies because they wanted to capture Rangoon before the monsoon season began. This would make many roads impassable and create difficulties for air supplies to be dropped. Slim was also mindful that the Japanese would probably put up a determined defence as they had elsewhere in the Far East and Pacific theatres of the war. This would be particularly so with Rangoon because of its strategic importance.

Slim's superior Lord Louis Mountbatten, Supreme Allied Commander of South East Asia Command, ordered that Rangoon be taken before 5 May 1945 and a planned attack known as 'Operation Dracula' was put into effect. Dracula was a combined amphibious and airborne assault on Rangoon where a Gurkha parachute battalion would land at the mouth of the Rangoon River and secure coastal batteries while naval minesweepers cleared the waters of mines. The 26th Indian Infantry Division, which included the Warwicks in the 4th Indian Infantry Brigade, would also advance on the city by establishing beachheads on both banks of the Rangoon River.

On 1 May 1945, 14 USAAF squadrons bombed Japanese defences in southern Rangoon before the Gurkhas in 50th Indian Parachute Brigade were dropped onto Elephant Point at the mouth of the Rangoon River. After several firefights with small groups of Japanese soldiers, the river approaches to the capital were captured.

Meanwhile, Kemp and the Warwicks were the first regiment on land to enter Rangoon although they did not encounter the expected heavy fighting. The Japanese Burma Area Army under the command of Lieutenant-General Heitaro Kimura had been stationed in Rangoon but most of his troops were not front line soldiers – they were instead mostly communications and naval personnel. Kimura decided not to defend Rangoon and launched an evacuation in late April. This was

British soldiers patrol through Burmese jungle and swampland during the advance towards Rangoon. Kemp recalls that marches like these were "a long slog"

Jim Kemp pictured during his army service. He was still in his teens when he fought against the Japanese

Two British Army soldiers patrol the ruins of Bahe during the Allied advance on Japanese-held Mandalay

BURMA CAMPAIGN

"SINCE 1941 BURMA HAD BEEN A HELLISH CHARNEL HOUSE IN WHICH THE ALLIES FOUGHT"

against orders issued by Field Marshal Hisaichi Terauchi of the Southern Expeditionary Army Group who demanded a fight to the death at Rangoon. Kimura defied this command because he wanted to hold on to his remaining forces.

It was during the conclusion of Operation Dracula that Kemp and his comrades heard about Victory in Europe. VE Day had occurred on 8 May but because of the distant lines of communication Kemp did not hear about the event until four days later on 12 May. Having just taken part in a major operation, Kemp could not comprehend the peace that had broken out on the other side of the world, "We didn't really want to know because we just had to keep doing what we had to in order to survive. Survival is one hell of a funny feeling at times and I'd often think to myself, 'Christ Almighty, how am I going to get out of this?'."

"Close-Quarters Fighting"

Operation Dracula had been an important event in the Burma Campaign, but Kemp's most significant fighting of the campaign took place afterwards. The Warwicks had been ordered to return to India on 20 May but three days later they found themselves fighting a small but desperate battle at Theinzeik, east of Rangoon.

Kemp was part of a small group of 24 British soldiers commanded by Major J. A. Collins who were patrolling along a dried-up river, "We had to form ourselves up into a reconnaissance patrol to find out where the Japanese were and what they were going to do. It was a quite a scary thing because we didn't know where we were going."

Collins's patrol suddenly encountered a large Japanese force that was later estimated to be more than 100 in number although Kemp did not know that at the time, "We were walking our patrol and the officer in charge said that we'd better stay where we were and do a recce to find the Japanese. We did that and then the officers announced that they wanted to sort out the Japanese there and then. We had gone out there as a reconnaissance patrol and finished up as a fighting patrol."

In an astonishing but desperate fight the outnumbered British achieved a small victory without any fatalities, "We didn't know we were fighting far more Japanese than us – not at all – but none of the British soldiers were killed. We just didn't know how many we were facing. We went in there with bayonets fixed and we had to go in and destroy them. It was close-quarters fighting and simple survival was going through my mind. The key to survival was that if you didn't kill the Japanese soldier in front of you then he would kill you. The Japanese wouldn't give in and they would never surrender."

For this action at Theinzeik, Major Collins was awarded the Military Cross, Britain's third-highest decoration for gallantry for his leadership. Other soldiers were awarded a Military Medal and a Mention in Despatches. The Warwicks as a whole who were serving in Burma were also commended by their divisional commander Major-General Henry Chambers.

The grim reality of hand-to-hand combat was a potent example of the vicious, determined fighting qualities of the Japanese and Kemp had to remain pragmatic despite the hardships, "We didn't really know how badly the Japanese would treat prisoners-of-war. You'd be told that the Japanese would kill rather than surrender themselves but what did that mean? It was just a few words but so many things would go through your mind. You couldn't imagine just walking through the jungle and suddenly being shot at. It was hard to understand how the Japanese could act like that and the best description I can make is that they would go into battle 'head-first'."

As well as the Japanese, Kemp also had to contend with extreme campaigning conditions in a vast, dense landscape, "The humidity and heat was constant but you had to cope with it. These were some of the main problems and of course where we were in Burma was covered in jungle. If you had been walking through the jungle for six or seven days you wouldn't know how far you'd travelled unless there was a landmark like a village or something similar. However, there were often no villages around with any information to tell you where you were. You had a map of course but you still often didn't know your location. Also, when we were advancing we would travel on foot for most of the way so it was a long slog."

In addition to the difficult terrain, the jungles of Burma were breeding grounds for debilitating tropical diseases. If soldiers became ill they had to continue, no matter how serious their condition, "I contracted malaria but it was nothing really, it just made you feel bad. I didn't get sent back [for treatment] so I had to keep going."

VJ Day and Indian Partition

The Warwicks eventually returned to India and were stationed there when the atomic bombs were dropped on Hiroshima and Nagasaki on 6 and 9 August 1945. For Kemp and his comrades, the brutal dawn of the nuclear age was received with relief as it spared Allied troops from fighting on mainland Japan, "It was good news to us because it did help to end the war and I'm sure that it actually saved a lot of lives although it killed thousands of people."

Japan surrendered five days after the bombing of Nagasaki on 14 August with Victory over Japan Day (VJ Day) occurring the following day. Kemp and his friends celebrated the end of the war but their festivities were muted by a supply shortage, "When the war ended I was back in India. We got the news that the war had finished and we celebrated with one bottle of beer between four of us. The three men I was with decided that the bottle we had should be kept somehow so we soaked the label off. I've still got it as a souvenir.

British troops in a landing craft make their way ashore on Ramree Island, 21 January 1945

Stuart light tank of an Indian cavalry regiment during the Allied advance on Rangoon

The interview for this article was conducted shortly before Jim Kemp sadly passed away in 2020. Jim was a member of the Royal British Legion (www.britishlegion.co.uk), Britain's largest military charity for veterans and their families. Jim was also a member of the Burma Star Association' (www.burmastar.org.uk), membership of which is open to all men and women who served in the Burma Campaign.

KEY BATTLE

IWO JIMA

After an arduous slog through the Pacific, US Marines mounted one final assault on Japanese forces in an attempt to unlock the mainland

WORDS JOSH BARNETT

IWO JIMA

Located 650 miles south of Tokyo in the Volcanic Islands cluster, Iwo Jima was home to two Japanese airstrips (with a third under construction at the north end of the island). The US believed this small island, just eight square miles in size, to be a strategic necessity for mainland attacks. If the island could be captured, the island would be used as a base for escort fighters, as well as a landing patch for damaged B-29 bombers returning from the mainland.

The Japanese had also recognised the importance of Iwo Jima and, under the command of General Tadamichi Kuribayashi, began constructing numerous inland bunkers in the summer of 1944, a noted departure from the usual beach fortifications used by the Imperial Japanese forces. US aerial and submarine reconnaissance showed the supposed scale, with 642 pillboxes, blockhouses and other gun positions identified prior to the assault.

A summer-long barrage designed to incapacitate the staunch Japanese defences ensued. For 74 days straight, US bombers pummelled this tiny blot of volcanic rock, while in the 72 hours running up to the invasion, the US Navy peppered Iwo Jima with shells, shattering the peace of this once idyllic South Pacific island.

The invasion begins

Codenamed 'Operation Detachment', the invasion proper began on 19 February 1945. The assault was tasked to the V Amphibious Marine Corps, led by General Holland 'Howlin' Mad' Smith, Commanding General for the expeditionary troops once ashore. H-Hour was set for 09:00, with the initial wave of armoured amphibian tractors coming ashore at 09:02 followed, three minutes later, by the first troop-carrying vehicles.

Spilling down the ramps, the 4th and 5th Marine Divisions (led by Major General Clifton B Cates and Major General Keller E Rockey respectively) waded through the ankle-deep volcanic ash of Iwo Jima's south-western shore unopposed. The pre-invasion bombardment appeared to have cleared the island. However, unknown to the US forces, Kuribayashi's 109th Infantry Division was holed up in a network of over 5,000 caves and 11 miles of tunnels around Iwo Jima, waiting for the landing force's shelling to cease before showing their resistance.

There were murmurs among the US troops that the Japanese forces had been wiped out as the beach remained eerily quiet – a marked departure from previous infantry battles in the Pacific where shorelines were staunchly defended. The landing plans tasked the 5th Division's 28th Regiment with taking Mount Suribachi, the 554-foot dormant volcano at the island's southern-most tip, by the end of D-Day. Likewise, the 4th Division was scheduled to take Airfield 1 the same day. In the calm of the initial landing, both plans seemed achievable yet, as the leading battalions crested the terrace at the end of the beach, General Kuribayashi gave the order to take up weapons.

The unmistakable chatter of machine gun fire from hidden Japanese emplacements cut down the initial waves of US troops, as artillery and mortar fire now began to pound the beaches. The soft volcanic soil, churned by the pre-invasion barrage, proved difficult to move through at pace, slowing the US advance. To make matters worse, fortifications on Mount Suribachi (protected by reinforced steel doors) rained down shells on the troops below.

"UNKNOWN TO THE US FORCES, KURIBAYASHI'S 109TH INFANTRY DIVISION WAS HOLED UP IN A NETWORK OF OVER 5,000 CAVES AND 11 MILES OF TUNNELS"

Despite landing some 30,000 men, progress was slow and, by the time the US advance was called to a halt at 18:00, the Marine line fell well short of their targets on the first day of the operation. Still, Mount Suribachi's north-eastern side had been surrounded by the 28th Regiment. The 5th's 27th Regiment had been able to push towards the north-western coastline but had taken heavy casualties in doing so. Meanwhile, the 4th Division skirted around Airfield 1's southern perimeter, securing a line towards the quarry near East Boat Basin.

During previous battles, Japanese banzai charges had caused considerable chaos throughout the night and, expecting similar attacks, US forces remained vigilant during darkness. General Kuribayashi did not believe in the usefulness of such tactics, though, feeling the banzai charge was a needless loss of life. This allowed the 3rd Battalion, 13th Marines (the artillery support for the 28th Regiment) to launch mortar and 105mm Howitzer shell attacks on Mount Suribachi during the evening of 19 February in preparation of an ascent the next morning.

Capturing Mount Suribachi

Formulated by the 28th's leader, Colonel Harry B Liversedge, the 2nd and 3rd Battalions plunged forward at 08:30 on 20 February, with the 1st Battalion remaining in reserve. With regular gunfire proving useless against the Japanese emplacements, US troops turned to their trusty flamethrowers and grenades to flush defenders out of their foxholes. However, the Japanese (thanks to their comprehensive tunnel network) soon re-manned each supposedly clear pillbox. It would be a tactic that kept US forces fighting on all fronts across the island, keeping the Marines' progress to a minimum.

Just 200 yards of Mount Suribachi had been taken by 17:00 on D+1. The following day, Liversedge's Marines attacked again after a

40-plane airstrike. With all three battalions heaving forward on one front, and with effective support from tanks and artillery, the 28th Regiment surged to the foot of the mountain. With the naval support covering the western side, the Marines had Suribachi surrounded by 22 February.

Finally, a day later, after reconnaissance from 2nd Battalion, a 40-man combat patrol was sent to the summit upon the orders of Lieutenant Colonel Chandler W Johnson. Under the command of First Lieutenant Harold G Schrier, they stormed the summit, raising a small US flag while under intense fire from the remaining Japanese troops. Later that day, a larger flag would be raised in order to boost the moral of the thousands of Marines across the island.

While the 28th Marine Regiment was still on Suribachi, the 26th and 27th Regiments of the 5th Division had pushed to Iwo Jima's western coast with suicidal rapidity, beginning their journey to the island's north sector on 20 February. Meanwhile, the 4th Division's 23rd, 24th and 25th Regiments had secured 'Motoyama 1', the southern-most airfield. With the 5th Division surging the Marine line forward by around 1,000 yards, only the 23rd Regiment (fighting on the 4th Division's left flank) could keep advancing at a similar pace.

Compared with the southern half of Iwo Jima, the northern sector was extremely well fortified, thanks to the efforts of Kuribayashi's men during that summer of 1944. The US Marines were finding the rocky terrain tough to negotiate, with every cleared pillbox and fortification soon reoccupied by Japanese forces, who were putting up a staunch and bloody resistance. Any gain the Marines made was seemingly met with renewed fire from the shellproof artillery emplacements and well-hidden tanks.

To aid the 4th Division's charge, General Cates called the 21st Regiment of the 3rd Division ashore on 21 February. However, with Japanese forces pinning down the 25th Regiment on the eastern shores, the beach was congested, forcing the 3rd Division's relief through the centre of the Marine Corps line in place of the 23rd Regiment. By the morning of the 22nd, frontline units were beginning to be relieved, with the fresh Marine forces able to grind out short territorial gains. Yet, Kuribayashi's men were alert to the fresh threat, pinning down units that were about to be replaced.

On D+4, V Marine Corps' Major General Harry Schmidt came ashore to survey the damage, ordering an attack the following morning. 24 February dawned with tanks thrusting through towards the second airfield, supported by the 21st Regiment. The 5th Division's tanks flanked Motoyama 2's western edge, while the 4th Division armour edged forward on the airstrip's east perimeter. Aided by a 76-minute naval bombardment, the US Marines were advancing once again.

Into the meat grinder

The same day, the remaining regiments of Major General Graves B Erskine's 3rd Division were committed to Iwo Jima. The veteran division was tasked with advancing through the supposedly flat centre line of the island, going head-on into Kuribayashi's main defensive line on 25 February. With flame-throwing tanks incinerating the enemy (and 50 per cent of the corps' artillery missions aiding the 3rd Division) three days of toil finally paid off on the evening of 27 February.

The US Navy Sixth Fleet photographed during the Battle of Iwo Jima

US Amtracs became stuck in the churned up sand of Iwo Jima's beaches

The Japanese line cracked, and the 9th Regiment found itself controlling two hills north of the second airfield, while the following day, the 21st Regiment stormed through the remnants of Motoyama village to seize two hills commanding over the unfinished airfield three. Elsewhere, the 5th Division had secured 'Hill 362A' after initial resistance from the Japanese proved deadly. 224 of the Division's Marines were killed or wounded on 1 March, but the hill's access to Nishi Ridge on the north-west edge of the island was too important to bypass.

While many hills had fallen with relative ease, Hill 382 on the eastern edge of the island was proving a more difficult proposition for the 4th Division. Honeycombed with Kuribayashi's tunnels, the hill's approach was guarded by hidden tanks, while the crest had been fortified into a huge artillery-proof bunker.

South of the hill was a series of ridges, topped by 'Turkey Knob', while further south of this massive rock was a natural bowl known as the 'Amphitheatre'. The fighting here was bloody, with 1 March the fourth day that the division's Marines had hurled themselves at the Japanese forces. Such was the relentlessness of this quadrant, it became known as the 'meat grinder'. It wasn't until 10 March that the Japanese defenders around 'Turkey Knob' were eliminated. Naval fire, carrier air strikes, heavy shelling and many Marine lives were needed before Hill 382 finally fell into US hands.

In this time, the 5th Division's 26th Regiment had succeeded in securing 'Hill 362B' on 3 March, before the 3rd Division readied itself for the assault on 'Hill 362C' four days later. Under cover of darkness (a departure from the usual US tactics in the Pacific), General Erskine's men

IWO JIMA

Once the US Marines established a beachhead, the gradual grinding down of Japanese resistance began

advanced beyond the unsuspecting Japanese forces. It was a blow for the General Kuribayashi, yet his men remained to resist strongly in their lasting areas of occupation.

Unfortunately for Imperial Japan, their attacks were becoming increasingly unco-ordinated, allowing patrols from the 3rd Marine Division to reach the northern coast by 9 March. The following evening, there was only one final pocket of Japanese resistance left in the division's sector, although the tunnels underneath the ground gave many more fanatical infantry a hiding place.

In the eastern sector, home of the 4th Division, Japanese troops launched a counterattack on 8 March. Under the cover of heavy artillery fire, the men attacked the Marine forces, worming their way through the 23rd and 24th Regiment's lines. Some attacked with the blood-curdling banzai cry, though many chose a stealthier approach, attempting to impersonate wounded US soldiers. Despite the counterattack's ingenuity, it was an ultimately hopeless effort that saw 650 Japanese killed by noon the following day. The end result was that, on 10 March, the Turkey Knob/Amphitheatre salient was completely destroyed as Marine forces pushed Kuribayashi's defences right back to the northern coast.

Clearing up the north

For the remainder of Operation Detachment, each Marine division would be faced with isolated pockets of resistance dotted around Iwo Jima. The 3rd Division was tasked with destroying a heavily fortified resistance south-west of Hill 362C (eventually achieved on 16 March), while the 4th Division focused on an enemy stronghold between East Boat Basin and Tachiiwa Point.

Across the island, 5th Division bore down on Japanese forces around Kitano Point, the last point of defence in the Iwo Jima campaign. Joined by two battalions of the 3rd Division's 21st Regiment, the final Marine drive began on 11 March with naval shelling and airstrikes. The US artillery again had little impact, though, making initial progress painstaking.

Despite being ravaged since the initial landing on 19 February, the 5th Division carved through 1,000 yards between 14-15 March, as many of the Japanese troops met a fiery end at the hands of the Marines' flame-throwing tanks. The following day, the 21st Regiment flanked the Japanese on the right, providing the US forces with two attack fronts to decimate the remaining Imperial forces.

By 25 March, organised enemy resistance was declared over. However, Kuribayashi's men made one final assault. In the vicinity of Motoyama 2, some 300 men assembled that evening. On the morning of the 26 March 1945, they stormed the US camp, killing sleeping Marines at will until a defensive line was formed by the Americans as dawn broke, sending the remaining Japanese into hiding. After 36 days, the Battle of Iwo Jima became a manhunt, with at least 223 Japanese soldiers tracked and killed. General Kuribayashi was rumoured to have been among those slain, bringing to an end a bloody conflict that saw more than 70,000 Marines deployed.

OPPOSING FORCES

US LEADER
General Holland Smith
US INFANTRY
1 Amphibious Corps (3 US Marine Divisions)
TANKS
c.150 M4A3 Sherman tanks (including 8 with the Mark 1 napalm flamethrower)
US GAME CHANGERS
The sheer number of men (around 70,000) thrown into battle over the course of the 36-day invasion.

JAPAN LEADER
General Tadamichi Kuribayashi
JAPAN INFANTRY
1 Imperial Infantry Division
TANKS
22 from Lieutenant Colonel Baron Takeichi Nishi's 26th Tank Regiment
JAPAN GAME CHANGERS
11 miles of tunnels, 642 pillboxes and 5,000 caves dotted around the island, along with the Japanese Infantry's tenacious defence.

General Holland Smith

General Tadamichi Kuribayashi

DUTCH VAN KIRK

Having served 58 missions in Africa and Europe during World War II, Dutch Van Kirk transferred to the 509th Composite Group. He was the navigator on the Enola Gay, which on 6 August 1945 dropped the first nuclear bomb on the Japanese city of Hiroshima. When he passed away in 2014, he was the only surviving crew member of the Enola Gay.

KEY EVENT

HIROSHIMA

The first atomic bomb was dropped on Japan by an American B-29 bomber, preceding the capitulation of Imperial Japan. Here one of the crew members of the Enola Gay, which dropped the bomb, recalls his experience of the day that changed history

WORDS **ADAM MILLWARD**

Theodore Van Kirk, known to everyone as 'Dutch', was having trouble sleeping. It was a common affliction among soldiers before a mission, but then again Dutch and his fellow 11 crewmates stationed on the tiny Pacific island of Tinian had more reason than most to be suffering from insomnia that night. The date was 5 August 1945 and tomorrow morning they were to drop the first-ever atomic bomb on Hiroshima.

To pass the time, some of the crew – including navigator Dutch, bombardier, Tom Ferebee, and pilot, Paul Tibbets, played poker. It was quite prophetic considering that in a matter of hours they would be gambling again – but this time with much higher stakes.

Sure, the USA had successfully detonated the first nuclear device the previous month during the Trinity test in New Mexico, and Dutch, like all the crew, had several months' intensive training at Wendover Airbase in Utah under his belt. Nevertheless the fact remained that what they were about to do had never before been attempted in warfare.

Indeed, Dutch recalls, "One of the atomic scientists told us we think you'll be okay if the plane is [14.5 kilometres] nine miles away when the bomb detonates." When challenged on his use of the word think, he levelled with them: "We just don't know."

Dutch had been hand-picked to join the 509th Composite Group – the unit tasked with deploying nuclear weapons – by his former commander: "I flew with Paul Tibbets all the time in England. We flew General Dwight Eisenhower [later to become US president] from Hurn [on the south coast of Britain] down to Gibraltar, for example, to command the North African invasion.

"Then we were all separated and doing various things – I was at a navigation school, for example, teaching other navigators. Tibbets was picked to take command of the 509th group and that's when he looked up some of the people he'd worked with in the 97th [Bombardment Group]."

The history books often paint a picture that the US government and other Allied powers were hand-wringing right up until the final hour over the decision to use the A-bomb. However, although Japan was presented with an ultimatum to surrender on 26 July – which they rejected two days later – Dutch personally felt it was always a foregone conclusion the bomb would be dropped: "I knew that I was going to drop the atomic bomb from February of that year [1945]. It didn't come as a surprise. We were posted to the US airbase at Tinian for about a month prior to dropping the bomb, just keeping in shape."

Around 10pm, the crew were called from the barracks to have breakfast before one last briefing and final checks of the Enola Gay. Dutch remembers they had pineapple fritters because he hated them, but Paul Tibbets loved them. While he might not have seen eye to eye with his commander when it came to breakfast, he has only praise for the man that piloted the specially modified B-29 to Hiroshima – and back again.

"He was an outstanding pilot. His skill saved all of the crew's lives a number of times in Europe and Africa. When he got in an aeroplane, he [became] part of it. When you flew with Paul Tibbets you didn't have to have your shoes polished or your pants pressed – and all that sort of stuff – but when you got in the plane, you better damn well know what you were doing!"

It's hard to imagine what the mood on the Enola Gay must have been like as it took off at 2.45am, but from Dutch's perspective this mission was the same as any other. "We were going a long distance over water, using Iwo Jima as a checkpoint on the way. Now if you got lost between Iwo Jima and Japan, you really were a sorry navigator! Everybody on board was doing his own thing. Ferebee took a nap, for example, [while] our radio operator, as I recall, was reading a whodunnit about some boxer. Everybody was making sure they did what they were there to do, and that they did it right."

While the Enola Gay and Bockscar (the plane that dropped the Nagasaki A-bomb) are the two that have gone down in history, Dutch is keen to point out that the operation was a lot wider than that: indeed, seven aircraft were involved in Special Bombing Mission #13 to Hiroshima on 6 August. Three were observational planes that flew ahead to ensure conditions were right, Top Secret was a backup to the Enola Gay which landed on Iwo Jima, while the other two aircraft – The Great Artiste and Plane #91 (later named Necessary Evil) – accompanied the Enola Gay for the full operation over Japan.

"The Great Artiste had instruments that were to be dropped at the same time as we dropped the bomb. If you were to ask me the name of them, I couldn't tell you; I just always called them 'blast meters' because that's what they were measuring. The other aircraft [Plane #91] was flying about [32 kilometres] 20 miles behind with a large camera to get pictures of the explosion. Unfortunately on the day the camera didn't work. So the best pictures we got were from the handheld camera of the navigator on that plane."

The three aircraft arrived at Hiroshima without incident around 8am. The city had been chalked as the primary target for several reasons. There were a great number of military facilities and troops there, as well as a busy port with factories supplying a lot of the materials that would be used to defend Japan in the event of an invasion. Beyond these factors, Hiroshima had never been previously targeted by Allied forces, so any damage recorded later could solely be attributed to the nuclear bomb. Tragically for the citizens of Hiroshima, it also meant the Japanese authorities had very little reason to suspect an attack there – even when the tiny squadron of three B-29s was no doubt spotted approaching.

On the actual bomb run, Tibbets relinquished control of the Enola Gay to bombardier and close friend of Dutch's, Major Tom Ferebee. As the Little Boy bomb (which actually was not so little,

> **"I DIDN'T FEEL TOO GOOD ABOUT DROPPING THE BOMB – BUT I DIDN'T FEEL TOO BAD ABOUT DROPPING IT EITHER. IT COULD HAVE BEEN US..."**

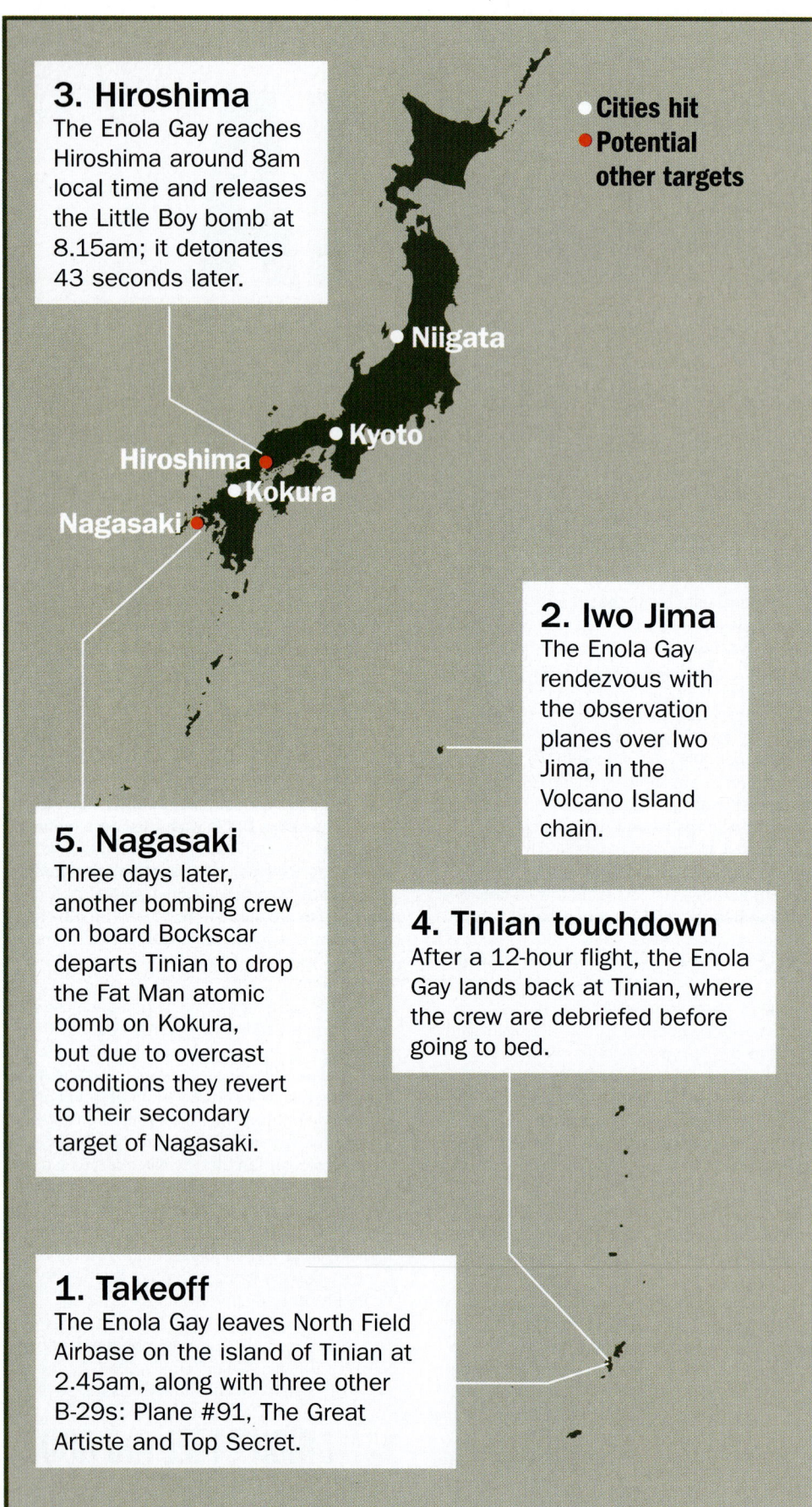

3. Hiroshima
The Enola Gay reaches Hiroshima around 8am local time and releases the Little Boy bomb at 8.15am; it detonates 43 seconds later.

2. Iwo Jima
The Enola Gay rendezvous with the observation planes over Iwo Jima, in the Volcano Island chain.

5. Nagasaki
Three days later, another bombing crew on board Bockscar departs Tinian to drop the Fat Man atomic bomb on Kokura, but due to overcast conditions they revert to their secondary target of Nagasaki.

4. Tinian touchdown
After a 12-hour flight, the Enola Gay lands back at Tinian, where the crew are debriefed before going to bed.

1. Takeoff
The Enola Gay leaves North Field Airbase on the island of Tinian at 2.45am, along with three other B-29s: Plane #91, The Great Artiste and Top Secret.

"WHEN WE TURNED TO LOOK BACK, ALL WE COULD SEE OF HIROSHIMA WAS BLACK SMOKE AND DUST"

weighing in at 4,400 kilograms/9,700 pounds) was released, the plane experienced an upward surge, but Tibbets managed to stabilise the B-29 and beat a hasty retreat.

"We made the 150-degree turn that we'd practised many times and pushed down the throttle to get away. All people were doing was holding on to something [in preparation for] the turbulence that was sure to follow. A loose person or a loose anything in the plane was going to go flying, so we all made sure we were in position and wearing our goggles." They were about 14.5 kilometres (nine miles) away when the bomb exploded, 43 seconds after it had been released. "We couldn't hear a thing over the engines, but we saw a bright flash and it was shortly after that we got the first shockwave.

"When we turned to take a look back, all we could see of Hiroshima was black smoke and dust. The mushroom cloud was well above us at about [12,190 metres] 40,000 feet and still rising. You could still see that cloud [480 kilometres] 300 miles away." What the crew of the Enola Gay couldn't have known at that point was just how destructive the atomic bomb had been. Underneath all that smoke and dust nearly 70 per cent of the city's buildings had been laid to waste and 80,000 people were dead – and that figure was set to rise with the much-underestimated effects of radiation.

Unlike The Great Artiste with its faulty camera, as far as Dutch was concerned on board the Enola Gay "everything had gone exactly according to plan. The weather was perfect; I could probably see Hiroshima from [120 kilometres] 75 miles away. My navigation was only off by six seconds," he says with pride. "Tom put the bomb exactly where he expected. We got a lot of turbulence, but the plane did not break up, which it could have done, and we got home. Now, as for the second mission to Nagasaki, everything went wrong. They had a lot of luck on that mission…"

Three days later, on 9 August, a different bombing crew on Bockscar almost didn't make it to Nagasaki due to a combination of bad weather and logistical errors. However, they managed to salvage the mission; the result of their success, or 'luck' as Dutch describes it, was the instant obliteration of another city and at least 40,000 of its inhabitants. Less than a week later, Emperor Hirohito made an unprecedented radio announcement to his subjects, declaring Japan's surrender due to "a new and most cruel bomb, the power of which is incalculable, taking the toll of many innocent lives."

A few weeks after the bombings, Dutch Van Kirk was part of the crew transporting scientists to Nagasaki to measure the devastation of one of these 'new and most cruel bombs' first-hand. "Having picked up some scientists in Tokyo from the Japanese atomic programme – they were also working on atomic bombs, you see – we flew down to Nagasaki; we couldn't land at Hiroshima at that time. We landed on a dirt field and the Japanese commander of the base came out, looking for someone to surrender to. We were given old cars – 1927 Chevrolet models, or similar – to drive to the city centre, but they all broke down three times before getting into Nagasaki.

"There wasn't really anything that shocked us, though there is one thing [that has stayed with me]. The Japanese military was being broken up at the time and one of the soldiers arrived on the bus

Seven of the Enola Gay's 12-man bombing crew stand before the aircraft; Dutch is third from the left, looking down, next to pilot Paul Tibbets

The North Field Airbase on Tinian played host to 15 modified B-29s and their crews

HIROSHIMA

COUNTDOWN TO DESTRUCTION

16 July 1945

5.29am — **First detonation**
US scientists successfully detonate the first nuclear device at the Trinity test site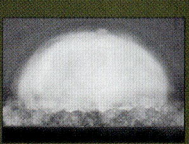

28 July

Japanese government rejects surrender terms put forward in the Potsdam Declaration

5 August

2pm — **Calm before storm**
Having been told they have the go-ahead to drop the atomic bomb, Van Kirk and the rest of the crew try to get some sleep

3pm — The Little Boy bomb is loaded onto the Enola Gay

6pm — Struggling to sleep, Van Kirk, Ferebee, Tibbets and others play poker

10pm — The crew gets up to prepare for the flight to Hiroshima and eat breakfast

6 August

12am — Van Kirk and the crew make their way to the Enola Gay, after a final briefing

1.37am — **Weather report**
The three weather planes leave North Field Airbase on Tinian to confirm conditions are favourable

2.45am — The Enola Gay takes off, followed by three other B-29s taking part in Special Mission #13

5.52am — **Little Boy armed**
The planes fly over Iwo Jima island, where the Enola Gay's backup, Top Secret, lands. The Little Boy bomb is armed

7.30am — With the all-clear from the weather planes, the Enola Gay, The Great Artiste and #91 head for Hiroshima

8.13am — Pilot, Paul Tibbets, hands over control to the bombardier, Tom Ferebee, to make the bomb run

8.15am — **Payload dropped**
Little Boy is released and it detonates 43 seconds after, about 600m (1,900ft) above the city of Hiroshima. The Enola Gay experiences a shockwave moments later

3pm — **Mission complete**
The Enola Gay touches down on Tinian, its mission successfully completed. Paul Tibbets receives the Distinguished Service Cross

looking for his home – but it had been destroyed. I remember looking at Tom Ferebee, and saying, 'You know, Tom, that could have been us if the war had gone the opposite way.' I didn't feel too good about dropping the bomb – but I didn't feel too bad about dropping it either. This was one man among many that were saved by dropping the bomb" – because it had precluded a full-scale invasion of Japan. "It was very important we saw that, and we both recognised how lucky we were."

Along with all the other Enola Gay crew, who have since passed away, Dutch Van Kirk has no regrets about dropping the atomic bomb, seeing it as the lesser of two evils. Asked whether he believes the result would have been the same – that is to say, the Second World War would have been forced to end – if things 'had gone the opposite way' and Japan had dropped an atomic bomb on America first, there's a long pause, before Dutch responds: "No, I don't think so. I think we would have been more resilient."

But underneath the assured bravado of his reply, there's no getting around how long he had hesitated before he answered – or the fact that, like that atomic scientist who couldn't offer any certainties on Tinian back in 1945, he had used the word 'think'.

The interview with Dutch Van Kirk that appears here was conducted in 2013 a year before Dutch passed away aged 93. To read more about and his story, pick up a copy of, *My True Course: Northumberland To Hiroshima* (2012, by Suzanne Dietz).

★ 2 SEPTEMBER 1945 ★

SURRENDER OF JAPAN

After two atomic bombs devastated Hiroshima and Nagasaki, the Emperor of Japan broke the news to his military and his people that the war was lost

On 15 August, 1945, Emperor Hirohito broadcast the news of Japan's surrender to Allied forces. Speaking over the radio, the first time an Emperor had addressed the nation in this way, Hirohito did not use the word 'Surrender', but instead referred to the need for unity and for the country to rebuild. "The enemy has begun to employ a new and most cruel bomb," he said. "the power of which to damage is indeed incalculable, taking the toll of many innocent lives." US President Harry S. Truman confirmed the capitulation later that day and large celebrations broke out across the world in a similar vein to the previous VE Day.

VJ Day marks the effective end of the Second World War, though sporadic fighting continued. The surrender ceremony for Japan's capitulation took place aboard USS Missouri on 2 September. Japanese representatives, including Foreign Minister Mamoru Shigemitsu and General Yoshijiro Umezu, Chief of the Army General Staff, signed the instrument of surrender, which was accepted by US General of the Army Douglas MacArthur on behalf of the Allies. Among the Allied attendees invited by MacArthur were two officers recently released from imprisonment by the Japanese: General Jonathan Wainwright, who had been captured at Corregidor during the invasion of the Philippines in 1942, and Lieutenant General Arthur Percival, who surrendered Singapore the same year.

SURRENDER OF JAPAN

The Japanese delegation arrived on the USS Missouri, 2 September 1945

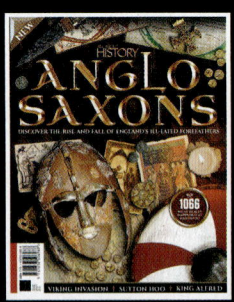
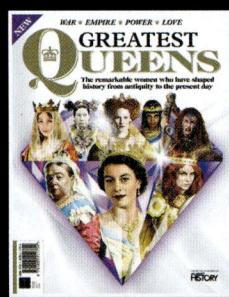
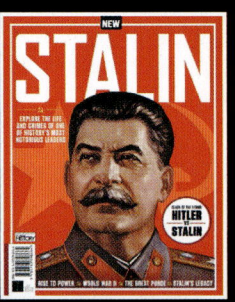
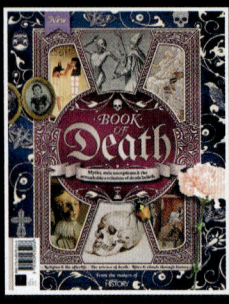
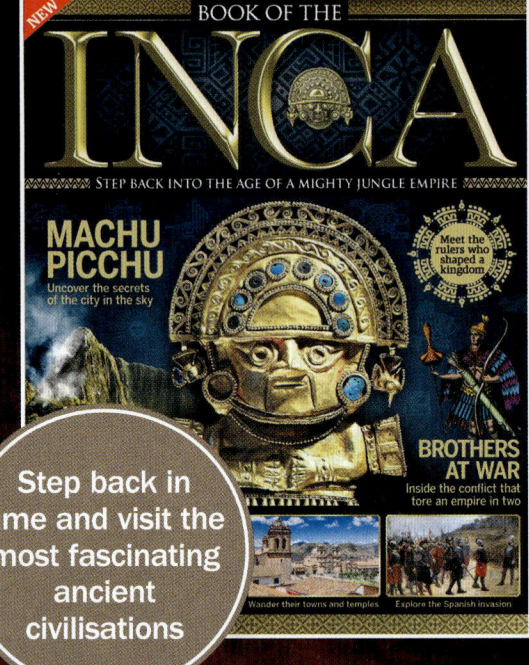

Examine world wars and epic battles through maps and rare documents

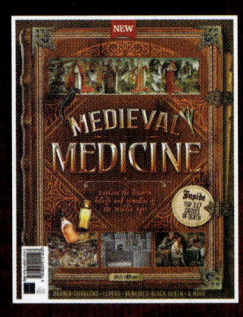

Step back in time and visit the most fascinating ancient civilisations

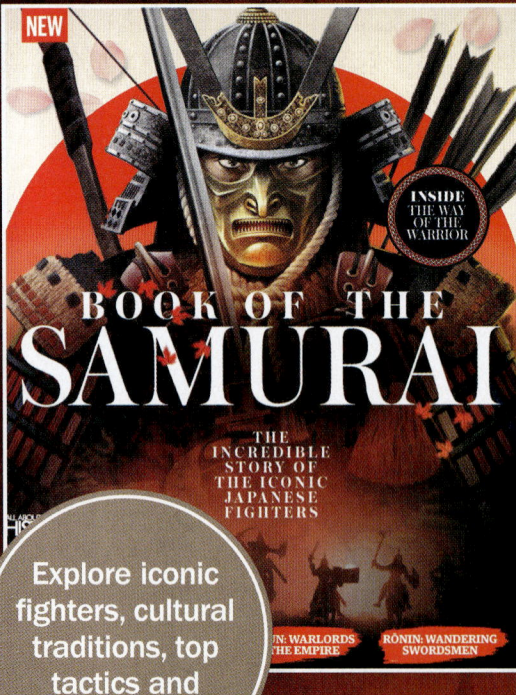
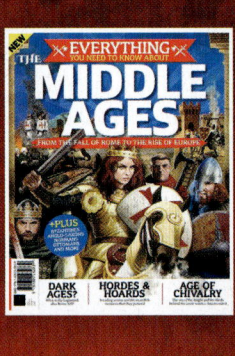
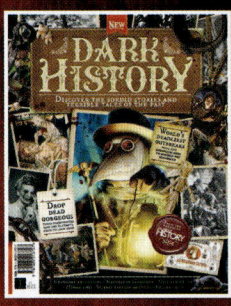
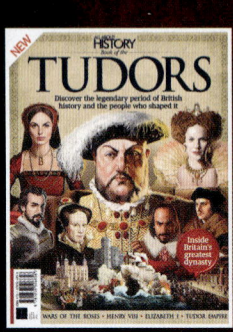
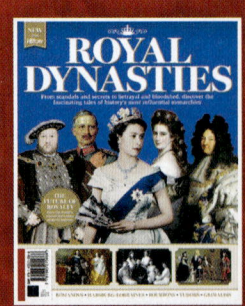
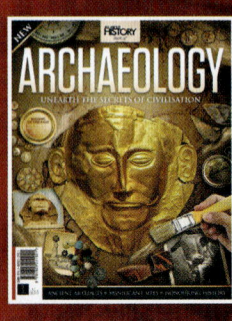

Explore iconic fighters, cultural traditions, top tactics and weapons

Get great savings when you buy direct from us

1000s of great titles, many not available anywhere else

World-wide delivery and super-safe ordering

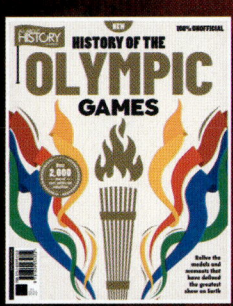
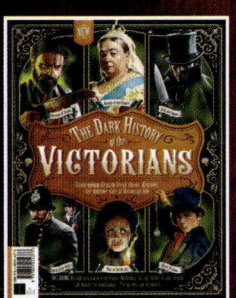
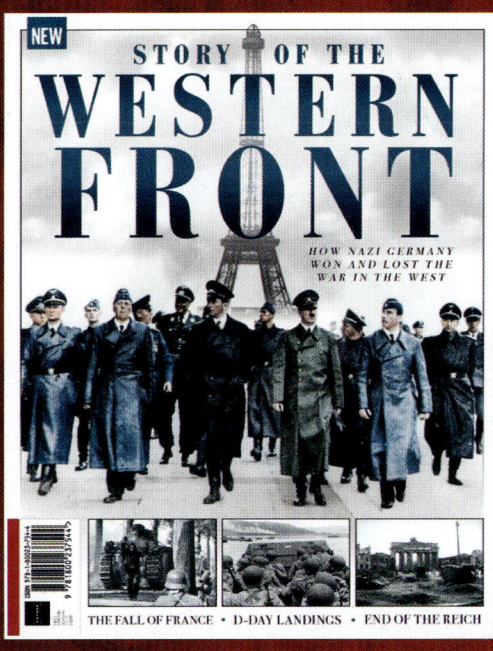
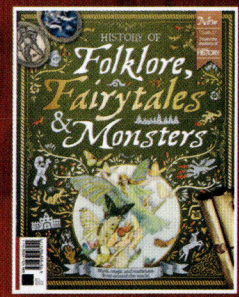
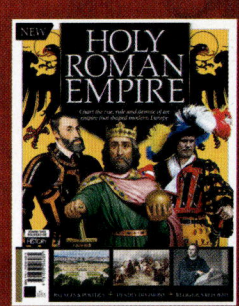
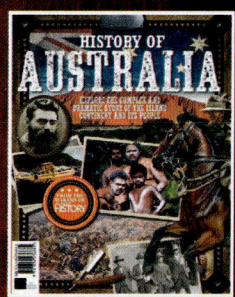
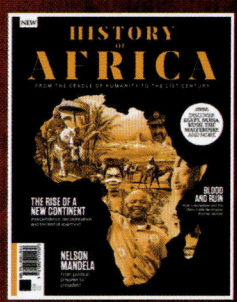

STEP BACK IN TIME WITH OUR HISTORY TITLES

Immerse yourself in a world of emperors, pioneers, conquerors and legends and discover the events that shaped humankind

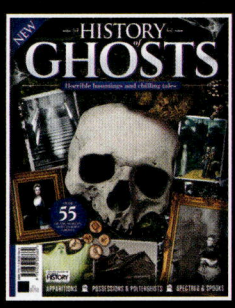

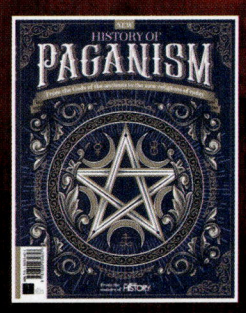
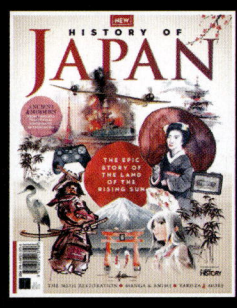
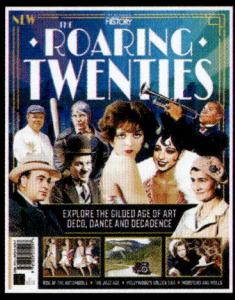

Discover the answers to history's burning 'what if' questions

Follow us on Instagram @futurebookazines

FUTURE

www.magazinesdirect.com/history

Magazines, back issues & bookazines.

★ WORLD WAR II ★
THE PATH TO VICTORY

Future PLC Quay House, The Ambury, Bath, BA1 1UA

Bookazine Editorial
Editor **Tim Williamson**
Designer **Perry Wardell-Wicks**
Head of Art & Design **Greg Whitaker**
Editorial Director **Jon White**
Managing Director **Grainne McKenna**

History of War Editorial
Editor in Chief **Tim Williamson**
Senior Designer **Curtis Fermor-Dunman**
Senior Art Editor **Duncan Crook**

Cover images
Adobe Stock, Alamy, Getty

Advertising
Media packs are available on request
Commercial Director **Clare Dove**

International
Head of Print Licensing **Rachel Shaw**
licensing@futurenet.com
www.futurecontenthub.com

Circulation
Head of Newstrade **Tim Mathers**

Production
Head of Production **Mark Constance**
Production Project Manager **Matthew Eglinton**
Advertising Production Manager **Joanne Crosby**
Digital Editions Controller **Jason Hudson**
Production Managers **Keely Miller, Nola Cokely, Vivienne Calvert, Fran Twentyman**

Printed in the UK

Distributed by Marketforce – www.marketforce.co.uk
For enquiries, please email: mfcommunications@futurenet.com

GPSR EU RP (for authorities only)
eucomply OÜ Pärnu mnt 139b-14 11317, Tallinn, Estonia
hello@eucompliancepartner.com, +3375690241

World War II: The Path to Victory First Edition (HWB6676)
© 2025 Future Publishing Limited

We are committed to only using magazine paper which is derived from responsibly managed, certified forestry and chlorine-free manufacture. The paper in this bookazine was sourced and produced from sustainable managed forests, conforming to strict environmental and socioeconomic standards.

All contents © 2025 Future Publishing Limited or published under licence. All rights reserved. No part of this magazine may be used, stored, transmitted or reproduced in any way without the prior written permission of the publisher. Future Publishing Limited (company number 2008885) is registered in England and Wales. Registered office: Quay House, The Ambury, Bath BA1 1UA. All information contained in this publication is for information only and is, as far as we are aware, correct at the time of going to press. Future cannot accept any responsibility for errors or inaccuracies in such information. You are advised to contact manufacturers and retailers directly with regard to the price of products/services referred to in this publication. Apps and websites mentioned in this publication are not under our control. We are not responsible for their contents or any other changes or updates to them. This magazine is fully independent and not affiliated in any way with the companies mentioned herein.

FUTURE
Connectors. Creators. Experience Makers.

Future plc is a public company quoted on the London Stock Exchange (symbol: FUTR)
www.futureplc.com

Chief Executive Officer **Kevin Li Ying**
Non-Executive Chairman **Richard Huntingford**
Chief Financial Officer **Sharjeel Suleman**

Tel +44 (0)1225 442 244

Part of the
HISTORY of WAR
bookazine series

Widely Recycled

ipso. Regulated